Trusting God in the Wilderness

Sin, Suffering, and Temptation
1 Corinthians 10:1-13

Lenten Reflections

Ted Wueste

Library of Congress Cataloguing-in-Publication Data
Wueste, Ted
Let Every Heart Prepare Him Room: Advent Reflections / Ted Wueste
Library of Congress Control Number: 2021922823

ISBN 9780991636884
1. Devotional. 2. Lent. 3. Spiritual Formation.

Printed in the United States of America
First Edition

CONTENTS

INTRODUCTION

As we journey through life, we often find ourselves in a desert kind of place. A place that feels desolate, lonely, harsh, and perhaps unfamiliar. And we might even feel the compulsion to escape and run to more familiar landscape. However, we are invited to resist that temptation for it is in those dry, desolate, lonely places that the Father does some of His best work. It is in those places where our souls become dry and thirsty that we are unwilling to settle for clichés and easy answers. The stripping and unmasking of the desert are so good for our souls. If we desire God, the wilderness is where transformation occurs.

The 40 days of the Lenten Season is an invitation to journey like Jesus did in His 40 days of temptation in the wilderness. In many ways, Jesus' wilderness time was a redemptive "redo" of the 40 years that the people of Israel spent in the wilderness. He faithfully endured temptation, danger, and fasting to model something for us. He was giving us an example of how to faithfully navigate the vicissitudes of life. In Lent, as we engage in a fast or discipline of some kind, we are following "in His steps." (1 Peter 2:21)

In 1 Corinthians 10, the Apostle Paul encourages us to learn from the example of the people of Israel and not do what they did. As we engage with God over these next 40 days, we are able to experience faithful response to God as Jesus did, (Hebrews 5:8) leaving behind the ways in which we are tempted toward the lack of trust that typified the people of Israel.

In these next 40 days, we will walk through this passage step by step:

> *For I do not want you to be unaware, brothers, that our fathers were all under the cloud, and all passed through the sea, and all were baptized into Moses in the cloud and in the sea, and all ate the same spiritual food, and all drank the same spiritual drink. For they drank from the spiritual Rock that followed them, and the Rock was*

Christ. Nevertheless, with most of them God was not pleased, for they were overthrown in the wilderness.

Now these things took place as examples for us, that we might not desire evil as they did. Do not be idolaters as some of them were; as it is written, "The people sat down to eat and drink and rose up to play." We must not indulge in sexual immorality as some of them did, and twenty-three thousand fell in a single day. We must not put Christ to the test, as some of them did and were destroyed by serpents, nor grumble, as some of them did and were destroyed by the Destroyer. Now these things happened to them as an example, but they were written down for our instruction, on whom the end of the ages has come. Therefore let anyone who thinks that he stands take heed lest he fall. No temptation has overtaken you that is not common to man. God is faithful, and he will not let you be tempted beyond your ability, but with the temptation he will also provide the way of escape, that you may be able to endure it.

1 Corinthians 10:1-13

Each week, we'll explore one of these situations which confronted the people of Israel. We will pray through issues like willfulness, idolatry, lust, doubt, pain, and suffering. That list may sound daunting, but God is "abundantly present" with us and will walk with us step by step on the journey as we navigate the terrain toward faith and trust.

Sundays are not traditionally included in the 40 Days of Lent and are usually a bit of a respite from one's fast or discipline. So, on Sundays, we will stop and pray through an examen prayer and celebrate the grace and love of God that we are noticing throughout the previous week.

As we enter into these 40 days together, let's begin by noticing desire. More than being rescued from the pain and finding life on the other side of the wilderness, let's begin by noticing the deeper desire to know God and trust Him in the wilderness.

Questions for reflection: are there ways in which you have located your desires outside the wilderness? Ask God what it might look like for you to be present in the wilderness with Him.

Prayer: Lord, by your mercy and through your grace, give me eyes to see that what I desire more than anything else is to know you and trust you. I entrust to you my pain, my confusion, my frustration and ask that I become more and more aware of your good presence with me. Amen.

Week One

From Expectation to Trust, vv. 1-5

Day 1 – Repentance   Ash Wednesday

As we begin this journey with God in the wilderness, we start on a day that has been set aside in the church for roughly one thousand years – Ash Wednesday. Today marks the beginning of this 40 Day fast leading up to Easter in which we are invited to intentionally enter a wilderness as Jesus did in Matthew 4. Ash Wednesday is an invitation to prepare our hearts for the journey. To stop and wonder about the path ahead. C. S. Lewis commented that lent is a season of "wonder that makes you serious." In this, we can move toward understanding the gravity of the wilderness because wonder means that we don't have it all figured out. Wonder is an invitation to ask: what I am being invited into? What do I need to notice? How is God at work in this season?

The specific invitation of lent is to engage in spiritual practices that will open ourselves to a gracious God who desires for us to be able to respond to Him with our whole hearts. More than anything, it is the practice of releasing our notions of "knowing" as we release our dependence on self and what we think we know. We release self-determined action and receive spirit-led response to God and what He is doing. As Jesus entered His 40 days, we read that "Jesus was led up by the Spirit into the wilderness." (Matthew 4:1)

This leads us to consider the Ash Wednesday practice of repentance. While the word repentance is often thought of in very harsh terms and may conjure up images of preachers holding signs on a street corner that say "repent" as they yell at people and their sinful ways, repentance is actually one of the most beautiful words in all of God's word. The Greek word for repentance means to have a change of mind. As we are moving down a certain path, repentance is the gracious invitation from God to see things differently and change our mind about our direction. In thinking about a journey, to repent is to realize that you are not on the right trail or path, to step off that path, and then to remember once again the path the Lord has designed for you.

But how do we know the path the Lord has designed? The prayer of Psalm 119:105 proclaims "Your word is a lamp to my feet and a light to my path." The imagery is clear that we can know the path through God's word to us, and the imagery of the lamp suggests that it is only enough light to see our feet and the path right before us. Certainly, there are many specific things that the Scriptures to do not address and this leads us to other half of knowing the path: through the Holy Spirit. The prayer of Psalm 143:10 requests "Teach me to do your will, for you are my God! Let your good Spirit lead me on level ground." The Holy Spirit may use God's word to prompt us toward us repentance or He may lead us through that quiet whisper we read about in 1 Kings 19. Either way, our response is to have a change of mind, to repent … to follow the leading of the Holy Spirit. In this way, repentance is indeed a beautiful invitation.

And, we might also say that repentance is a way of life. We are invited to constantly notice and listen, step off the path, and remember or reorient. This is a rhythm and a spiritual muscle we can develop. And, that repentance muscle is so needed in the wilderness. In a space or season where we are frequently confused, often discouraged, and sometimes angry, the gift of being able to notice the Spirit's leading and adjust the way we are walking is "grace upon grace."

In Ephesians 5:1, we are encouraged to "walk in love as Christ loved us." However, there are so many obstacles on the journey and the Apostle Paul challenges us to "awake, O sleeper" (vs. 14) because of the very real possibility that we are sleepwalking without an awareness of where we are and what the heart of God is for us. In the very next verse, we read "Look carefully how you walk" (v. 15) which is followed by "be filled (or, led) by the Spirit." (v. 18)

Based on this, let me suggest a repentance rhythm of reflect, release, and remember. When we noticed we've fallen asleep (i.e., not walking in love), we can awaken as we reflect on what's going on in our hearts, release that which is not love or trust, and remember the path that honors the heart of God and our design.

Question for reflection: are there ways in which you have been sleepwalking? Ask the Spirit to search your heart and show you ways you have not been on the path.

Prayer: Lord, today, give me eyes to see those places where I can repent. I thank you for your kindness in repentance and invitation to come back over and over again. Give me strength to live into the truth of who I am. Amen.

Day 2 – 1 Corinthians 10:1-5

A wilderness season is usually not something we would have expected. While we know difficult seasons can come, they are generally not on our bucket list. What we usually expect is that our lives will be fun and satisfying. While we may not consciously think about it this way, this is what is often happening in our hearts. The deep work of God in the wilderness is to lead us through expectation into deepening trust.

While the people of Israel seemingly did everything but trust God in the days of their exodus from slavery in Egypt, God's heart was to nurture trust in them. They had been shaped in particular ways in their years of bondage and the journey through the desert was the gift of being re-formed and transformed into the kind of people who would flourish in the land of promise.

Like the people of Israel, we may have idealized notions of what the promised land is like. We hear "flowing with milk and honey" (Exodus 3:8) and may hold expectations that milk and honey are just there for the taking to enjoy. However, milk (coming from goats who fed on the often-fickle grasses of Canaan) and honey (which would be found here and there as the environment was fruitful) are both images that represent an abundance that was dependent upon rain. Unlike a lush, tropical paradise, the weather was inconsistent and unpredictable. Truly, it was a land of promise but it was a place of deep faith and trust.

In the journey from Egypt, God took them into the wilderness where water and food were in short supply if any was to be found at all. Why would God do this? Because He loved them and was shaping them for life with Him. In many ways Egypt had shaped their hearts and minds away from trust. Being slaves, they would have had no trust in or love for their masters. In addition, they had been shaped to expect that their lives were in their own hands. If they were going to make it, it would not be because the "system" cared for them but because they knew how to work within it. Finally, as slaves, any sense of worth or identity would have been rooted in what they could accomplish and how well they could perform for the Egyptians.

Read how their wilderness journey started …
For I do not want you to be unaware, brothers, that our fathers were all under the cloud, and all passed through the sea, and all were baptized into Moses in the cloud and in the sea, and all ate the same spiritual food, and all drank the same spiritual drink. For they drank from the spiritual Rock that followed them, and the Rock was Christ. Nevertheless, with most of them God was not pleased, for they were overthrown in the wilderness. (1 Corinthians 10:1–5, ESV)

They had all the spiritual resources needed to experience the transformation of the wilderness just as we do. They were delivered from slavery to Egypt … we are delivered from slavery to sin. They were "baptized" into Moses … we are baptized into Christ. They were given the cloud to guide them … we are given the Holy Spirit. They had spiritual food and drink … we have the bread and wine of communion.

God had taken them out of Egypt and now he wanted to take Egypt out of them. The wilderness would have reshaped their hearts, if only they had let it. In Christ, we are given all the spiritual resources we need to experience formation into people of deepening trust, walking in love … and it is a journey. It means releasing expectations and the ways we've been shaped to think life works. Releasing is not easy work. It is often painful and disorienting.

Author Gerald May wrote, "Expectations are premeditated resentments." Unexamined and unseen, our expectations can lead us toward all the same resentful responses that were present for the Israelites: anger, discontent, fearfulness, and striving.

I first taught through this passage 25 years ago, and at that time, I called the teaching "Out of the Wilderness." Now, I see more clearly that it is not about ***getting out***, but trusting God ***in*** the wilderness. My expectations had been that God was supposed to get me out of difficult seasons and that a difficult season couldn't be the plan. Examining our expectations is one of the first steps on the journey of deepening trust.

Questions for reflection: in what ways are you (or, have you been) in a wilderness season? What expectations might the Spirit be leading you to release? What are the invitations to trust?

Prayer: Lord, give me the wisdom to release expectations and ways I've been shaped that do not lead to trust and love. I need your wisdom to know what trust looks like right now. I want to trust, and I also confess that often I don't. Thank you for the ways you are at work in me, leading me. Amen.

Day 3 – Matthew 4 – Jesus learned obedience

Jesus "learned obedience through what he suffered." (Hebrews 5:8) It may sound odd to say that Jesus needed to learn obedience, but it starts to make sense as we understand the nature of obedience. The word itself may sound harsh to many ears and certainly the concept of obedience has been used to manipulate and abuse. However, in the Gospels, obedience is connected to love and trust, "if you love me, you will keep my commandments." (John 14:15) Of course, the word "commandment" is often thought of in harsh terms as well, but the commandments of God, as described in the Scriptures and especially the Psalms, are seen differently. In particular, Psalm 119 records, "I find my delight in your commandments," "Your law is better to me than thousands of gold and silver pieces," and "your precepts have given me life." The commandments of God are not oppressive but freeing, precious, and delightful.

Obedience is a loving, trusting response to God. God doesn't desire for us to just conform to some rigid list of moral standards. He desires for us to walk with Him in love and trust. His commandments give us discernment for walking the path of love. They are a compass that guides us into loving response to the God who loves us. So, in what way did Jesus learn obedience? While He was perfect and continually in fellowship with the Father and the Spirit, an obedient response in the context of His humanity was something that had to be learned, or experienced. In the wilderness of Matthew 4, Jesus' responsiveness to God the Father was tested and it is no coincidence that in each of the three temptations He responded with Scripture.

Hebrews 4:15 tells us we have a great high priest who has been "tempted *just* as we are" … tempted to take matters into His own hands, tempted to escape the wilderness, tempted to define His life outside relationship with the Father. Make no mistake, for Jesus the 40 days of wilderness were a time of vulnerability and danger. Mark 1:13 notes that Jesus "was with the wild animals, and the angels were ministering to Him." He was fasting during this time as well which would have had its own sense of vulnerability.

When we are in a wilderness season, God's heart is that we would "learn obedience" as well, that we would experience a deep sense of trusting responsiveness to Him. Our responsiveness is tested significantly when we are left without our usual resources for making life work. Whether a health crisis, a relational crisis, or perhaps a financial crisis, one of the temptations is to redouble our efforts … to go to those old ways of managing life once again, trying harder. The reality is that all of our efforts don't solve the problems and we are often left wondering if we can trust this God who is leading us and showing us the way. The stripping down and the emptiness of the desert can feel far more vulnerable and dangerous than we believe we can stand. Robert Mullholland suggests that "Like the Hebrew people in the desert [we long] for the comfort and security of Egypt. [We cry] out to God, 'Did you bring me out here to kill me?' The answer of course, is yes."

Yes? Really? God, you want me to be stripped down to nothing? You want me to die? And, if we are willing to be that honest … that willing to bring this question to God, we might just simply hear those words of Jesus: "For whoever would save his life will lose it, but whoever loses his life for my sake will find it." (Matthew 16:25) It is when we are willing to be in the wilderness space, vulnerable to all that it brings that we find the life that is truly life. As we let go and release trying to make things work, we find that, like Jesus, we are learning deeper responsiveness (or, obedience) to God.

It can feel lonely in this place and that is by design because, as Adele Calhoun writes, "Solitude is a formative place because it gives God's Spirit time and space to do deep work. When no one is there to watch, judge and interpret what we say, the Spirit often brings us face to face with hidden motives and compulsions. The world of recognition, achievement and applause disappears, and we stand squarely before God without props."

Finally, because of the loneliness and disorientation, we can find ourselves in a place of resistance, still not sure that we are interested. Are there ways you find yourself resisting the wilderness? Consider the counsel of the prophet Isaiah, "And though the Lord give you the bread of adversity and the water of affliction, yet your Teacher will not hide himself anymore, but your eyes shall see your Teacher. And your ears shall hear a word behind you, saying, "This is the way, walk in it," when you turn to the right or when you turn to the left. (30:20–21)

Question for reflection: how might the Teacher be speaking to your heart and pointing out the path to walk along? Pause and listen. Ask God to speak to you in this wilderness season.

Prayer: Lord, I am willing to abide with You in the wilderness even though I feel resistance. I want to trust that You are up to something good … for Your glory which is also what I desire. Give me strength to listen, to notice how You are with me and leading me. Amen.

Day 4 – The Voice in the Wilderness is Love

In the wilderness, there is a quiet produced by the stripping away. It can be wonderful, and it can also be maddening. One of the reasons that God takes us into the wilderness is to speak to us. It is in the quiet that we can hear His still small voice. It is also in the quiet that we may begin to notice things in us rising to the surface … things that had been suppressed or stuffed down by the noise of life as we'd known it. In Hosea 2:14, God speaks to the people of Israel, "Therefore, behold, I will allure her, and bring her into the wilderness, and speak tenderly to her." He is never forceful or demanding but gentle and inviting. We hear His voice as we embrace the wilderness and all that it brings.

Listening and hearing from God is often a struggle. In speaking of what happened in Israel's wilderness journey, God says in Psalm 81:11-13:

> "But my people did not listen to my voice; Israel would not submit to me. So, I gave them over to their stubborn hearts, to follow their own counsels. Oh, that my people would listen to me, that Israel would walk in my ways!"

God will not force us, and He will not shout over all the other noise. He desires so deeply for us to hear His tender voice … to listen to His heart more closely than the other voices that we might believe will give us clarity. The challenge for us can be a "stubborn heart," or in the words of Psalm 95, a "hardened heart." What might a hardened heart look like? Put very simply, we might say that it is a heart which is tuned in to other voices … for example, the voices of the past, the voices of expectation, the voices of other people. When we are listening to these voices, it can be noisy and frustrating, especially if we desire to hear the voice of God. But God never stops speaking. He is always present and always communicating.

The invitation is to detach from the other voices. Hardness of heart becomes a factor when we are attached to the other voices, when we have given them the space to lead us and take us off the path. The goal is not to necessarily get rid of other voices but to release them

… to not hold on to them. The other voices may linger but the noise lessens when we are no longer trying to manage them or control them or indulge them. We can do this by practicing a prayer of quiet. We simply sit quietly, seeking to be present to God's presence with us. As various thoughts or impulses come into our awareness, we let them float on by like driftwood in a stream and center our attention again on God's presence with us.

Over time, the voice of the Lord and our awareness of His presence becomes clearer and clearer. What we hear and what we begin to notice (often in ways that are beyond words, cf. Ephesians 3:19) is that He is present and that He loves us.

This brings us back to the third part of the rhythm of repentance: remembering. As we *reflect* on the various voices that may have our attention and then *release* them, God graciously speaks to us the truth of His love and our call to that path of love.

When everything else is gone, we find that we are left with love. And what we realize is that His love is enough. His love is our sustenance, our identity, our reference point. To try to define the love of God can be difficult because it is something beyond knowledge. At the same time, we might best equate it with the word "presence." He will never "leave you nor forsake you." (Hebrews 13:5). Jesus said, "I am with you always, to the end of the age." (Matthew 28:20) The name Jesus, given before His birth, was Immanuel which means "God with us." Presence … His abiding presence … is His love. As we grow in the awareness of His presence, we become more and more grounded in His love.

And it is presence in the midst of the mess … in the middle of the wilderness. It is not something we experience after things are cleaned up or when we have act together, but something now. The very things (our sin, our failings, our distractions) which we have believed keep us distant from God become the points of connection. Jonathan Maury, SSJE, says it so well: "Through repentance and faithful belief in the good news, we acknowledge our own failings – which become the paradoxical means to union with God and one another through Jesus' call."

As we reflect and release, then we begin to *remember* the truth. The truth that He is with us. He loves us. He sings over us with joy and quiets us with His love. (Zephaniah 3:17) The one who is leading us is the One who is always present … always loving … always speaking to us.

Questions for reflection: are there other voices to which you listen? What is it like for you to consider that God speaks to you tenderly? How might you begin to detach from other voices so you can more clearly hear the voice of love?

Prayer: Lord, I want to listen to Your voice above any others. I desire to live in Your love. Give me eyes to see that You are singing over me with joy. Amen.

First Sunday
Remember God's Goodness in the Previous Week

On Sundays, we are invited to pause in order to remember God's goodness and His work in us on the journey thus far. In Psalm 106, the history of Israel's time in the wilderness is recounted and it is said that they "forgot his works" (vs. 13) and "they forgot God" (vs. 21). Remembering is vital for abiding with God on the path of love.

Use the following to engage in a time of examen prayer:
- Begin by quieting your heart before God and simply taking a few deep, slow breaths as you remember that you are in God's presence.

- Review the week with gratitude. What is the Spirit bringing to your awareness?

- Notice the ways that God has been present to you in the previous week.

- What are you thankful for? What might God want you to see that you didn't previously notice? Perhaps a place to repent?

- Select a part of your reflection from the week to pray over.

- Pray for the coming week.

Write out a prayer of thanksgiving and celebration as you look back and look forward.

Week Two

From Independence to Dependence, v. 6

Day 5 – Numbers 11:4-9

As we continue to consider the movement from expectation to trust, we now turn to the first example we are given 1 Corinthians 10. In verse 6, we read: *"Now these things took place as examples for us, that we might not desire evil as they did."* This may seem like a general statement of what happened in the wilderness and that is likely part of what is going on here. However, the wording here also suggests a reference back to Numbers 11 where it was written: "the rabble that was among them had a strong craving." The words "strong craving" are interesting when you examine the Hebrew language in which they were originally written. Literally, the two words are "desiring desire," and the idea is intensity as the word desire is doubled. Hence, the word "strong." Other English translations offer "wanton craving."

To be clear, desire is a good thing. We were designed with desire. Desire is what shapes us and motivates us. At our core is desire for God, but there may be other desires that have built up over the years to the point where our desire for God is almost unnoticeable. One of the reasons that God brings us to the desert is to expose desires that have become more prominent than our desire for God. The word that Paul uses in 1 Corinthians for desire is a compound word that literally means "over-desire" or intense desire, much like the doubling of the word "desire" in Numbers 11. In other contexts, it is translated as "lust."

The danger of this "over-desire" is that it is desire that is misdirected. If we think about desire having an object, like an archer would aim at a target, "over-desire" is desire that aims at the wrong target. This kind of misdirected desire is shaped by and directed toward evil. This is how the Apostle Paul explains it in 1 Corinthians 10:6 with phrase "that we might not desire evil." Evil is one of those words that we may resist. No one wants to think that they desire evil. We may think: *evil describes dictators from previous generations or serial killers, but not me!*

Part of such a response results from not fully understand desire. G. K. Chesterton once wrote, "Every man who knocks on the door of the brothel is looking for God." Underneath every desire is our desire for God. The goal is not to get rid of desire but to redirect it. In addition, evil is another one of those words that may need some redefining. It can be helpful to think about goodness. What is good? Simply put, good is that which is experienced in the context of trusting, loving relationship with God. As we listen to God and trust what He says about life and trust how He is leading us, we are living in the good. Micah 6:8 famously walks us through the question, "What is good?" The answer is justice and mercy as we walk humbly with God. Often, people identify with the first two elements and forget about the third. However, the third part is the linchpin … it is what effectively leads us into the other two. Walking humbly with God, we might say, is the essence of goodness. In contrast, evil is not walking humbly with God … not trusting His heart and what He has to say about life and love. Evil would be defining things on our own … living independently of God. This is what the serpent in Genesis 3 was leading our first parents toward … "you can't trust God. He's holding out on you. He is trying to manipulate you."

Essentially, we might say that the contrast between desiring evil and desire goodness can be understood respectively as independence from God and dependence upon God. We see this displayed in the words of Psalm 106, *"But they soon forgot his works; they did not wait for his counsel. But they had a wanton craving in the wilderness." (vv. 13-14)*

A note of caution: we often focus on *sins* as actions instead of looking at *sin* which is an independent heart which can stir and shape the desire for sinful actions. Not that actions and behavior are insignificant, but in the desert, God is leading us to look at our hearts, to examine desire. Two more notes of caution: it is not our responsibility to determine what is going on in someone's else heart (Matthew 7:3-4); and we also must take evil actions seriously (Isaiah 5:20). However, on the road of our own transformation, it is *our* heart that is the focus. Indeed, following Christ is a journey of the heart.

In the wilderness, we are often tempted to focus on behaviors and actions. Perhaps, this is simply another way to stay in control or live independently from God. We may be tempted to try to figure out what we need to "do" in order to get things back to normal, but it is examining our hearts that leads to the freedom and transformation for which we long.

Maurice Nicoll asks the question, "Why should a [person] leave the familiar and go into a wilderness? … [because] without temptation, there is no transformation." Wilderness can both surface misdirected desire as well as be the context for redirecting it.

Questions for reflection: As we move on this path from independence to dependence, are you willing to be uncomfortable? Are you willing to walk through the suffering rather than trying to fight it? Are you willing to look at your heart and desires instead of simply your actions?

Prayer: Lord, today, give me the strength to abide with you in the wilderness, noticing my heart and seeing misdirected desire. As I see, I trust you to reshape the direction of my desires. Amen.

Day 6 – Interacting with Desire

Let's go back to Egypt! The food out here in the wilderness is horrible. Back in Egypt, the food was great, the vegetables were fresh, and it was all free!

Wow! Quite a response from people in the wilderness (Numbers 11:4-6) They had been in slavery and had been led by God into freedom. Now, their desires (strong cravings) seemed to be getting the best of them. In the pain, confusion, doubt, frustration, and deprivation of the wilderness, their unformed, misdirected desires were shaping their response of *let's go back.*

It sounds so ridiculous until we realize that we often respond in the same way. When we find ourselves in the desert, we look for answers and comfort, and *our desire* directs where we go. In what can feel like an automatic response, we overeat, drink too much, indulge in fantasy, grumble, snap at others, or perhaps fall into despair when hurting. When life doesn't make sense, we can begin to sleepwalk into misdirected desire. The beauty of the wilderness (if you'd be willing to think about this way) is that we see those temptations more clearly. We see where those desires can take us. Getting angry when we are hungry has a name: hangry.

Jesus encountered hunger in the wilderness. Matthew 4:2-3 explains Jesus' experience: "After fasting forty days and forty nights, he was hungry. And the tempter came ..." (Matthew 4:2-3) To say He was hungry after 40 days is perhaps the understatement of all understatements, and it demonstrates that He was vulnerable and truly tested. It was in that moment that the tempter came. When we experience temptation in the wilderness, we can choose to engage it as a gift from God, an opportunity to grow deeper and closer to Him. Indeed, "without temptation, there is no transformation."

So, how do we do this? In temptation, we often end up distancing ourselves from God, thinking that we have to *get it together.* What does it look like to draw near? Let me suggest a few things:

First, don't suppress desire. Desire is a beautiful, powerful thing. When desire is suppressed, it becomes more powerful under the pressure. Pay attention to your desires because they are telling you something. To ignore desire is to let it run rampant in the corners of our unconscious self. Look at desire (holy, unholy, or unknown) and notice what is truer and deeper. Discern how an "unholy" desire is really a desire for God. Curtis Almquist, SSJE suggests: "Our desires are worth listening to. They do need to be brought into the light. Many of us – certainly I – need help sifting through our life's desires to see where they need to be deepened or purified, where they are connected to God's gift of life for us."

Second, pray your desires. Let God shape and redeem them. In the Psalms, we see our forefathers in the faith wrestling with God in prayer. Some of the things we observe in their prayers would certainly not be classified as "pure" desires, but it is bringing desire to God that sanctifies desires. Robert L'Esperance (SSJE) shared: "One of the best pieces of spiritual advice I ever received from a spiritual director was to pray for anything that I desired, even if that desire seemed sinful. It was a kind of 'prayer shock therapy,' designed to break through dualistic thinking patterns and begin integrating prayer with life as we actually experience it, rather than as we might wish it to be."

Third, practice gratefulness. Many of our misdirected desires are a result of jealously and lack of gratefulness. The last of the Ten Commandments from Exodus 20 encourages us to let go of covetousness. Covet is a desire word, and it means that we are desiring someone else's life. It is perhaps no coincidence that after the challenges to be honest and honor others, the capstone of the ten deals with gratefulness and desire. Arthur Simon shares: "When things are valued too much, they lose their value because they nourish a never-satisfied craving for more. Conversely, when things are received as gifts from God and used obediently in service to God, they are enriched with gratitude. As sages have said, contentment lies not in obtaining things you want, but in giving thanks for what you have." Experiencing gratitude can include our wilderness seasons and the struggles with desire. God is doing something that we can trust and, dare I say, even celebrate.

Jesus said, "come and rest" (Matthew 11:28-30) and we find rest as we learn His *way of being* which He described as gentle and humble. Gentleness and humility are perhaps two sides of the same coin. Gentleness is strength under control ... we might even say it is desire under control. Humility is the acknowledgement that God alone can direct our desires and strengths. As you experience desire today, practice humility by not suppressing, by praying, and by expressing gratitude. The result? A gentleness that leads to peace and rest!

Questions for reflection: what are some desires that you might pray? How might you trust God by bringing your desires to Him rather than waiting for the desires to (magically) go away?

Prayer: O Lord, I come to you with humility and give to you desires that I know are not your plan for me. I give you desires that I am uncertain about. I ask that you would shape these desires in the context of our time together. Amen.

Day 7 – When Manna from Heaven Is Not Enough

Part of the tragic irony in Numbers 11 is that God was graciously and miraculously providing for His people. Each morning, manna (some sort of seed/grain that could be crafted into bread) appeared on the ground. God had demonstrated His provision in delivering them from bondage in Egypt and now they were having a difficult time appreciating His provision of manna.

This manna from heaven was not enough. It failed to live up to their expectations. In Psalm 23, we are told the Lord is our shepherd and that this reality leaves us in a place of having "no want." However, we often find ourselves having a hard time seeing the provision, and instead we compare it with our previous *provision* or our expectations of what life would be like. At a foundational level, God always provides what is truly needed to live a life of dependence. Let that sink in for a moment. He gives us what we truly need to live a life of dependence. How often do our ideas of provision have more to do with living in such a way that we are independent and self-sufficient as opposed to vulnerable or dependent upon God?

In Isaiah 58:3, we observe this dynamic as the people of God fasted (entered into a wilderness of sorts) and asked: "Why have we fasted, and you see it not? Why have we humbled ourselves, and you take no knowledge of it?" The Lord responds by saying: "Behold, in the day of your fast you seek your own pleasure and oppress all your workers." What can subtly creep into our lives is a kind of transactional theology. *God, I'll do this (fasting, prayer, service) so that I get that (my ideas of the good life).* It's a transaction. God never promises this kind of relationship. What he promises is Himself, and our invitation is to move toward trust and dependence.

A few verses later in Isaiah 58, we read: "and the LORD will guide you continually and satisfy your desire in scorched places and make your bones strong; and you shall be like a watered garden, like a spring of water, whose waters do not fail." (v. 11) The questions that surface in the wilderness are: can I trust? Will he really provide? Can I put all my eggs in this one basket?

The questions are answered as we wrestle with the idea of satisfaction. What do I believe will truly satisfy me in this life? Is He enough? Is His provision enough? If we can be honest enough to say that *God is not always what satisfies me,* then we're making progress. It starts with wrestling with what we really believe and then it progresses as we actually wrestle with God. We can hold all the right "beliefs" and never see those beliefs worked out in the reality of our experience. How do we wrestle with God? Quite simply, in prayer. Perhaps our prayers might sound like this …

God, I want to trust You, but I don't.
Lord, these other desires feel stronger and more powerful than my desire for you.
Father, I desire You, and yet I also desire to find my satisfaction in my work.
Jesus, help me. I feel so dissatisfied. Give me eyes to see your provision.

As we experience misdirected desires, the invitation is to bring them to God in prayer. As we bring ourselves to God over and over, our response to desire begins to be: God Himself. Our desires begin to be directed toward Him. This is often a messy process and not for the fainthearted. We see this modeled over and over again in the Scripture. We see it in Jesus. Before Jesus went to the cross, He agonized in prayer. He prayed His desire: "Father, if you are willing, remove this cup from me. Nevertheless, not my will, but yours, be done." (Luke 22:42) The apostle Paul had a thorn in his flesh and he wrestled with God. He didn't know if the desire was misdirected or not, so he simply prayed. What he heard from God was: "My grace is sufficient for you, for my power is made perfect in weakness." (2 Corinthians 12:9)

God reshaped and reframed desire for Paul. First, with the reality that God's grace (His love, His presence) was enough for Paul. Second, with the truth that weakness or dependence is where power is experienced. It wasn't just believing the right things but hearing them from God in listening prayer … a dialogue in which we share and then listen. This happens, not as we try harder or simply believe the right things, but as we wrestle with God in prayer.

Alan Jones puts it so well: "A human being is a longing for God and nothing less than God will satisfy us; the seductive voices that would make us anything less than this are to be resisted."

Question for reflection: can I be honest enough to say that God is not always what I desire? Can I bring that to Him?

Prayer: Father, I bring all of who I am to you … all of my desires. I desire You, and I also don't desire You. What do you want to say to me? Amen.

Day 8 – Releasing Shame

As we consider misdirected desires and bringing them God in prayer, we may encounter a sense of shame. Asking questions like *Am I worthy?* or *What's wrong with me?* are quite common. And yet, God is not asking those questions. His posture toward us is that of grace upon grace. Romans 5:1-5 describes the salvation life that we have in Christ as one of hope, and "hope does not put us to shame, because God's love has been poured into our hearts through the Holy Spirit who has been given to us."

Hope (or, confidence) emerges from suffering … a time in the wilderness. Notice the progression in Romans 5:3-4: "we rejoice in our sufferings, knowing that suffering produces endurance, and endurance produces character, and character produces hope." As we walk with God through the wilderness, not trying to escape our circumstances or our desires, it leads us to hope. And, the hope is specifically a confidence that we can draw near to God. No matter what our experience may be, He receives us in the same way He received Jesus in Matthew 3:17: "this is my beloved son in whom I am well pleased."

Sit with this for a moment … God is pleased with you. In Christ, you have been adopted as a *beloved* child. (Galatians 4:5-6) Don't let this pass by too quickly. In many communities, the idea of being pleasing or displeasing to God is used over and over again, and we may use it as a grid through which we look at our life with God. The truth is this: *with YOU, God is well pleased*. He receives you and loves you beyond your capability to fully understand. Certainly, there may be desires or actions that are not pleasing to God, but you are not your behavior and you are not your thoughts. There is something deeper and truer about you as one made in the image of God and called His beloved.

How do we move this forward from a place of head knowledge to lived experience and identity? It happens as we actually relate to God with all of who we are. As we pray our desires (even the misdirected one), we connect with a God who loves us and receives us. What is incredibly pleasing to God from a "behavior" standpoint is when we choose to draw near to Him … and not a "drawing near" with thinking, believing, desiring, and doing all the right things, but coming to Him as we are … in need of a Father. At the core of God's heart is a desire for us to experience closeness to Him. The truth is that we could never be any closer to God than we are at this moment, but we are often unaware of that presence.

With shame, we can tend to avoid or hide … desiring to get things cleaned up and figured out before we come close. As we become aware again that we have distanced ourselves, shame emerges once more. And so, this "cycle" of shame illustrates the need to move from independence (*I'll get things together* or *I'll deal with this on my own*) to dependence (*I need God and will seek Him in prayer*).

The wilderness lays bare to us the reality of our hearts and our inability to deal with our "stuff" on our own. Deuteronomy 8:2-3 explains this beautifully, "Remember how the Lord your God led you all the way in the wilderness these forty years, to humble you and test you in order to know what was in your heart, whether or not you would keep His commands. He humbled you, causing you to hunger and then feeding you with manna, which neither you nor your ancestors had known, to teach you that man does not live by bread alone but on every word that comes from the mouth of the Lord." This may not be what we expect but it is how God works. It is certainly no coincidence that Jesus quoted the last part of verse three when He was in His wilderness experience.

Thomas Keating observed: "Our expectations of becoming paragons of piety, great contemplatives, attaining higher stages of consciousness – all subtly aimed at carrying us beyond the daily troubles of ordinary life – are not the way into the kingdom. Rather the kingdom consists in finding God in our disappointments, failures, problems, and even in our inability to rid ourselves of our vices."

We rejoice in our sufferings, knowing that they can lead us into the confidence to approach Him with no shame. The wilderness is harsh, and it is also a place where we draw close to the heart of God like never before … if we choose to be with Him in it.

Questions for reflection: are there ways that you can see shame at work in your life? What might be the invitation to release your shame?

Prayer: Lord, I am grateful to be Your beloved and to have the ability to draw near to Your heart. Give me eyes to see and then release shame when it is at play in my life. Amen.

Day 9 – Delight in the Lord (in the Wilderness)

Another barrier in the movement from independence to dependence can be trying to wrap our brain around what is going on. When things aren't making sense, we have a tendency to go to what we know … the familiar. For the people of Israel, the wilderness was filled with confusion, uncertainty, and discomfort. So, they longed for the familiarity and certainty of Egypt, even bringing themselves to think of it as a paradise compared to what they were experiencing. The invitation into deepening dependence is often accompanied by uncertainty whereas needing to understand everything is frequently a sign that we desire our independence. How do we get our bearings when we notice this struggle in ourselves? How do we jettison this barrier?

First, it can be helpful to remember that God's ways are not our ways (Isaiah 55). If we are uncertain about what is going on and we are aware of that uncertainty, then we are paying attention. In both Ephesians 3 and Philippians 4, we are told of a "love that surpasses knowledge" and a "peace that surpasses understanding." In Him, we have access to love and peace, and yet we can't think our way into experiencing them.

Second, we are wise to consider the counsel of 2 Corinthians 3:16-18: "But when one turns to the Lord, the veil is removed. Now the Lord is the Spirit, and where the Spirit of the Lord is, there is freedom. And we all, with unveiled face, beholding the glory of the Lord, are being transformed into the same image from one degree of glory to another. For this comes from the Lord who is the Spirit." Transformation happens as we behold God, not as we understand Him. Certainly, there are many things we can and need to understand about God but a shifting and changing of desires occurs as we behold. And what does it mean to behold?

In Psalm 27:4, David provides some insight, "One thing have I asked of the LORD, that will I seek after: that I may dwell in the house of the LORD all the days of my life, to gaze upon the beauty of the LORD and to meditate in his temple." To behold is to gaze and meditate. Psalm 37:4 develops this further in using the word "delight." "Delight yourself in the LORD, and he will give you the desires of your heart." This verse has often been read in a transactional way: *if you delight in God, He will give you what you want.* However, the word for "give" is better understood as the idea that God will instill desires in us, or we might even say "shape our desires." Here's the point: what we gaze upon or delight in will shape us.

Not only does a desert season reveal our hearts, it also reveals God's heart if we are looking … or if we are delighting. We see this in the verses from Deuteronomy we looked at yesterday: "Know then in your heart that, as a man disciplines his son, the LORD your God disciplines you." (Deuteronomy 8:6)

What do you hear as you read this? The word *discipline* may seem harsh, especially if we have received abusive kinds of discipline in the past. However, in this verse God is revealing His father-heart. The heart of a father delights in his children. He is for us, He loves us, He provides what is best for us, and the list could go on. God's *discipline* gives us an insight into the beauty of what can happen in the desert. As things are stripped away and we experience loss, His peace and love can become more real, more integrated into our hearts and lives. God, in His delight and love for His children, will lead us into spaces where our hearts can be shaped in ways that we could never imagine or even ask for.

Delight opens us to trust and receive a good Father's love in the midst of wilderness. Alternatively, when we are enmeshed in our thoughts and understanding, we may see our wilderness as a harsh punishment or that we've been abandoned by God. We might ask ourselves: am I delighting in God or trying to make sense of what is going on around me?

How do we delight in God? First, we can *meditate* on the reality that He delights in us. Our delight is always a response to His delight. Can you set aside some undistracted time and space to simply gaze upon the goodness and grace of God toward you? Seek to remember all the ways He has been present with you. Ask Him to help you see and then gaze, behold. Second, we can engage in *wondering* what kind of good/beautiful things God must be up to in the midst of the desert. We may have no idea and even be confused, but as we wonder with God it sets us in a space of waiting and watching.

"My soul waits for the Lord more than watchmen in the morning … for with the Lord there is steadfast love, and with him is plentiful redemption." (Psalm 130:6-7)

As we develop a habit of delighting in God in the quiet spaces, it overflows into our daily living and gives us eyes to see His love and His redemption.

Questions for reflection: what might God be up to in your life? Take some time to imagine with God how He is with you and shaping your heart. What do you notice?

Prayer: Lord, I am ready to let go and release my understanding of how things ought to work and seek to gaze upon Your beauty and meditate in Your presence. Give me eyes to see your goodness and mercy. Amen.

Day 10 – Hope is a Person, Not a Place

As you consider what was going on with the people of Israel, you can almost hear them whispering to one another, "This is not what we signed up for!" The Lord told them they were on the way to the promised land and that had become their hope. In their minds, what they were experiencing was certainly not part of the plan. Notice how Moses describes this:

"And you murmured in your tents and said, 'Because the LORD hated us he has brought us out of the land of Egypt, to give us into the hand of the Amorites, to destroy us. Where are we going up? Our brothers have made our hearts melt, saying, "The people are greater and taller than we. The cities are great and fortified up to heaven. And besides, we have seen the sons of the Anakim there."' Then I said to you, 'Do not be in dread or afraid of them. The LORD your God who goes before you will himself fight for you, just as he did for you in Egypt before your eyes, and in the wilderness, where you have seen how the LORD your God carried you, as a man carries his son, all the way that you went until you came to this place.' Yet in spite of this word you did not believe the LORD your God, who went before you in the way to seek you out a place to pitch your tents, in fire by night and in the cloud by day, to show you by what way you should go." (Deuteronomy 1:27–33)

Rather than seeing the love of God, they actually thought that God must hate them. Of course, if you sat them down and had a theological discussion, they might *know* the right answers but this was how they were experiencing the wilderness. "God hates us. He wants to destroy us." At times, we may also find ourselves in this kind of place. Our cancer, our failing marriage, our depleted bank account, or some other wilderness encounter may leave us wondering the same things. Did God save me to let me experience such difficult things? This is the abundant life? Really? This is not what I signed up for!

In Deuteronomy 1, Moses contrasts their response with the encouragement: "do not be in dread." Why? He explains:
- *The LORD your God who goes before you*
- *(He) will himself fight for you*
- *the LORD your God carried you, as a man carries his son*

What is he saying here?

First, *God leads us and He takes the initiative.* He doesn't leave us to fend for ourselves. We may feel alone but we aren't. He is leading us somewhere. As we consider the wilderness, we remember that He is taking us *from* something *to* something, and He always takes us *through* something … *from, through, to.* We like the "from" and the "to" … it is the "through" that can trip us up. God does not work by magic, transporting us to a new situation and location. He graciously (even if painfully) leads us "through." The journey is about deepening our dependence on Him. Why? Because *dependence* is the promised land. Hear that clearly. A life of dependence is the truest, most real hope in our lives. Our hope is Him, not some location outside of difficulty. It is experiencing Him and trusting Him in the wilderness that forges a dependence and reliance which is what we long for.

Father Pedro Arrupe expresses this beautifully: "More than ever I find myself in the hands of God. This is what I have wanted all my life from my youth. But now there is a difference, the initiative is entirely with God. It is indeed a profound spiritual experience. To know and feel myself so totally in God's hands." Is this your hope? What might it be like to fully embrace Him as your hope? Hope is a person, not a place. Have you set your sights on heaven (or some other earthly paradise) as your promised land or on Him as what you have wanted all your life?

Second, *He fights for us.* A common refrain throughout the Scriptures is God saying: "I will never leave you or forsake you." (Hebrews 13:5; Joshua 1:5; Psalm 37:25; 2 Cor. 4:9) He is with us and He fights for us. Because He is the one who has taken the initiative and goes before us, we can trust that He is leading the way in whatever situation we find ourselves. For those who are in Christ, Jesus is described as the forerunner, the one who goes before us. He fought for our redemption, and He keeps on fighting for us. "Consequently, he is able to save to the uttermost those who draw near to God through him, since he always lives to make intercession for them." (Hebrews 7:25) He is always praying for us and loving us. Sit with that for a moment.

In Hebrews 6:19, hope is described as an anchor for the soul. It is a beautiful metaphor for the way that hope keeps us tethered. Hope keeps us on the path. Hope is described as "entering into the inner place behind the curtain." This "inner place" is a reference to the Holy of Holies in the Temple of God. It is the place where we experience direct and complete access to God. Our hope is God Himself.

Finally, *He tenderly carries us, as a man carries his son, all the way through the wilderness.* We return again to the imagery of a tender father. He carries us *through*. He is faithful in His love for us ... to lead us to that place of dependence which ends up transcending space and time.

Part of the pruning in the desert is an *awareness* that our hope has been situational and circumstantial and then the *movement* toward our hope being *the life that we have with God ... right now, in the middle of the wilderness.* To engage in this kind of hope, let's revisit the repentance rhythm of reflect, release, and remember.

Reflect: in what ways has my hope been in other than the abiding presence of God?
Release: gently let go of those hopes.
Remember: *your life is hidden with God in Christ.* (Col 3:3)

Question for reflection: what would it be like to simply sit quietly and prayerfully with God, releasing other hopes and resting in His presence? (no words, just presence)

Prayer: Lord, You are my hope. It is You and the life we have together. Give me the strength to simply release other hopes that I might rest in your presence. Amen.

Second Sunday
Remember God's Goodness in the Previous Week

On Sundays, we are invited to pause in order to remember God's goodness and His work in us on the journey thus far. In Psalm 106, the history of Israel's time in the wilderness is recounted and it is said that they "forgot his works" (vs. 13) and "they forgot God" (vs. 21). Remembering is vital for abiding with God on the path of love.

Use the following to engage in a time of examen prayer:
- Begin by quieting your heart before God and simply taking a few deep, slow breaths as you remember that you are in God's presence.

- Review the week with gratitude. What is the Spirit bringing to your awareness?

- Notice the ways that God has been present to you in the previous week.

- What are you thankful for? What might God want you to see that you didn't previously notice? Perhaps a place to repent?

- Select a part of your reflection from the week to pray over.

- Pray for the coming week.

Write out a prayer of thanksgiving and celebration as you look back and look forward.

Week Three

From Striving to Rest, v. 7

Day 11 – Exodus 32

In the coming movement through the wilderness, God graciously and kindly desires to reveal more and more of our heart to us. While the terrain can be quite harsh on this journey, it is foundational to remember that it is His "kindness that leads us to repentance." (Romans 2:4) Repentance is that beautiful rhythm of reflect, release, and remember which is invited as we see those parts of our heart that would lead us astray. In the overall journey from expectation to trust, this week we come to the specific movement: from striving to rest.

Striving is an energy which is grounded in the impulse that we have to control whatever is going on around us. In the cherished verse from Psalm 46, God encourages His people to "be still (or, cease striving) and know that I am God." Why? If you read through the previous verses, you see that war and destruction was all around. The imagination of the people had gone wild, and they really believed that their world was falling apart. And what do we do when we perceive that things are out of control … that we've lost all semblance of power? We tend to run to things we believe will help us regain a sense of equilibrium, a sense of control.

In 1 Corinthians 10:7, Paul writes: "Do not be idolaters as some of them were; as it is written, 'The people sat down to eat and drink and rose up to play.'" The issue of the heart we are encouraged to explore this week is idolatry. For most of us, idolatry is not something on our radar. Compared to our observations of the ancient world, idolatry may not be as recognizable in our modern world because objects of false worship are generally regular, familiar parts of our everyday existence. But even for the ancients, what seems odd to us was regular and familiar to them, and the dynamics at the heart level were the same as what we experience today. Idolatry is so dangerous because it can be hard to detect.

The incident to which Paul refers in 1 Corinthians is found in Exodus 32:1-6:
"When the people saw that Moses delayed to come down from the mountain, the people gathered themselves together to Aaron and said to him, 'Up, make us gods who shall go before us. As for this Moses, the man who brought us up out of the

*land of Egypt, we do not know what has become of him.' So Aaron said to them,
'Take off the rings of gold that are in the ears of your wives, your sons, and your
daughters, and bring them to me.' So all the people took off the rings of gold that
were in their ears and brought them to Aaron. And he received the gold from their
hand and fashioned it with a graving tool and made a golden calf. And they said,
'These are your gods, O Israel, who brought you up out of the land of Egypt!'
When Aaron saw this, he built an altar before it. And Aaron made a
proclamation and said, 'Tomorrow shall be a feast to the LORD.' And they rose
up early the next day and offered burnt offerings and brought peace offerings. And
the people sat down to eat and drink and rose up to play."*

It's easy to see what is going on in this passage, and yet harder to see
how this might be at work in our own lives. The people had grown
impatient. How often are we impatient with the work of God in our
lives? How often to do we want we want … *now?* God may seem
slow, but His timing is always perfect. We can trust in the slowness of
God because He is our provider and will never leave us or forsake us.
Impatience is something we might notice as an issue when idolatry is
at work in our lives. And it can also be an invitation to seek God's
heart so that our desires would be furthered shaped by Him. Sit with
these questions for a few minutes … where does your mind tend to
go when impatience arises? Where do you tend to look when
impatient?

An idol is a false god as opposed to the true God of the universe. We
were created and designed to live in a dependent relationship with
God (consider our reflections from last week) as the one who is
everything … the sovereign One, the powerful One, the loving One,
the holy One, the omniscient One. When seeking our independence,
we gravitate toward things that will give us a personal grasp of those
same things … control, power, love, holiness, knowledge, etc. When
God isn't coming through the way we thought He might or when we
thought He would, we look for other sources of the things that only
God can provide. Without careful observation and reflection, we
might not see that this is what is occurring because we can be on
autopilot.

We simply go to what is familiar, what seems tangible, what we believe has come through for us in the past. We see this dynamic at play in Isaiah as God invites them to rest in trusting quiet:

> *For thus said the Lord GOD, the Holy One of Israel, "In returning and rest you shall be saved; in quietness and in trust shall be your strength." But you were unwilling, and you said, "No! We will flee upon horses"; therefore you shall flee away; and, "We will ride upon swift steeds"; therefore your pursuers shall be swift.* (30:15-16)

In their response, they chose familiar, tangible strength and power (horses were symbolic of power and strength in the ancient world). The contrast could not be clearer between striving to maintain control, power, and security and resting in God's strength that comes through trust and quietness. With the words *your pursuers shall be swift*, God graciously reminds them that "worshiping/trusting" in the gods of this world put us in a vicious cycle. True worship comes from a heart at rest.

Confronting the idols in our lives is not easy work and we often fail, but there is grace. Just a few verses later, Isaiah reminds: "Therefore the LORD waits to be gracious to you, and therefore he exalts himself to show mercy to you. For the LORD is a God of justice; blessed are all those who wait for him." (Isaiah 30:18) The word *wait* brings us back again to the concept of patience. For what do you need to wait?

Questions for reflection: do you see the tendency to run to things that might give you a sense of control and power and significance? Ask God to give insight into what this might be for you.

Prayer: Lord, thank You for always pursuing my heart and desiring what connects most clearly with how You've made me. This week, please give me courage and wisdom to reflect well on how idolatry is at work in my life, to release what I've been trusting that isn't You, and to remember that I can wait on You because Your timing is always perfect in all things. Amen.

Day 12 – False Self/True Self

Idolatry might be most succinctly and helpfully understood with the following: "if I can just do, have, or be this, I will be happy." Instead of God, what we think will make life work is what we do, what have, or what image we are able to project to the world. Generally, we might not even have the awareness to say it so directly, but this is often what is going on in our hearts.

And when undetected, for those who are in Christ, we can end up putting this "idolatry" into our relationship with God. In a sense, we can *idolize* God in an attempt to get our own independence and self-fulfillment through what we do, what we have, and what others think of us. Rather than a life of depending on Him/surrendering to His heart, we may view Him as one who can get us what we want. Of course, what we most desire is a life of dependence, but lesser desires are often more intensely at play.

For the people of Israel, the text of Exodus 32:6 is tragically fascinating. Aaron, the brother of Moses, had just built the golden calf. Then, he pronounced, "these are your gods that delivered you from Egypt," and announced that the next day they will have a feast to the Lord. The word "Lord" is the Hebrew word *Yahweh* which was the personal name of God. There are two things to note. First, they were attributing their release from captivity to these false gods. Second, they were mixing the worship of those gods with worshipping the one, true God.

Let's pause right here. Are there ways that you attribute things in your life to yourself? to your hard work? to whatever? Or, do you see yourself as completely dependent upon the vine who is Christ? (cf. John 15:1-5) Next, ask God to search your heart. Are there ways that you have combined worship/surrender to God with other pursuits? Again, pause here for a few moments as you listen and explore with God. He is gracious and will meet you where you are.

In Deuteronomy 8:17–19, we read: "Beware lest you say in your heart, 'My power and the might of my hand have gotten me this wealth.' You shall remember the LORD your God, for it is he who gives you power to get wealth, that he may confirm his covenant that he swore to your fathers, as it is this day. And if you forget the LORD your God and go after other gods and serve them and worship them, I solemnly warn you today that you shall surely perish." It is distinctly possible that we end up worshipping the gift rather than the giver. John Piper challenges us:

> "The greatest adversary of love to God is not his enemies but His gifts, and the most deadly appetites are not for the poison of evil, but for the simple pleasures of earth. For when these replace an appetite for God Himself, the idolatry is scarcely recognizable, and almost incurable." (*A Hunger for God*)

The temptation of mixing our worship of God with the pursuit of other things also includes a beautiful invitation because when we *reflect* on how we are tempted to be shaped by what some have called the false self, we have an opportunity to *release* and *remember* in trust and worship. More specifically, the false self is what we have been discussing: identifying ourselves with three things – what we do, what we have, and what others think of us. We can "use" God to prop these things up. Graciously, God waits, abides with us and beckons us, quietly and non-forcefully, to release and look fully at His provision … to rest in the reality that He is enough.

These three elements of the false self are the same things that showed up in Adam and Eve's temptation in Genesis 3 as well as Jesus' temptation in Matthew 4. For Adam and Eve, it was in the silence and joy of the Garden, and for Jesus, it was in the wilderness. And in both, temptation was presented in the context of their lives with God. Notice the parallels of these temptations:

- make one wise | get the kingdoms of the world | what I do
- fruit is good for food | turning stones to bread | what I have
- delight to the eyes | throw self down | what others think of me

In his book *Basking in His Presence*, Bill Volkman offers that the temptation contrasted with the invitation is about knowing (possessing) and unknowing (faith). "Like Adam and Eve, we all have been given the same basic commandment: 'From any tree of the garden you may eat freely; but from the tree of the knowledge of good and evil you shall not eat.' But, like Adam and Eve, most of us continue to make the mistake of choosing to eat of the fruit of the tree of knowledge, or tree of *knowing*, instead of in faith taking from the Tree of Life, the Tree of *Unknowing*."

Can you allow yourself to be in that place of unknowing … of trust? The idolatry of the false self is centered around garnering and possessing what we need rather than trusting God as our provider.

Over the next three days, we'll look at each of these parts of the false self and what it might mean to move from a place of striving into rest where we are increasingly freed to worship God alone. It is out of the "enoughness" of God that our true self emerges.

Questions for reflection: is God *alone* enough for me? In what ways would you say yes? In what ways would you say no?

Prayer: Lord, today I confess that in particular ways … dependence and trust in You alone has not been enough for me. And I desire deeply to live into worshipping You *alone* more and more. Thank you for the grace of letting me be in process along the way. Amen.

Day 13 – What We Do

When it comes to the deep soul work of the wilderness, we experience losses that can be incredibly disorienting. The ways our lives have been defined are no longer in place, and the things we thought we knew have been removed. The comfort of knowing what would happen next, even as the people of Israel were enslaved in Egypt, was stripped away and replaced with the unknowing and uncertainty of following God in the dry, dusty desert. While it feels harsh, it is love.

In Soul Making, Alan Jones observes: "The task of love is to help us rid ourselves of the exoskeleton, to lay us bare, to set us free. But we love the prison house. The place of bondage is, at least, familiar. Love, then, comes as an unwelcome shock." We may love the prison house because it gave us a sense of identity. When God rescues us from being enslaved to things other than Himself, He is doing it to bring us back to remembrance … remembering that we are not machines whose existence is defined by how many bricks we can make and how fast we can make them … remembering that we are designed and created to live fruitful lives that spring out of our life with God in which He alone is enough for us. For the people of Israel, they were shaped over centuries to believe that their worth was rooted in what they could do, what they could accomplish. We may find that have we been shaped in similar ways. It may have been family pressures to "make something of your life" or the societal pressures in which we are seemingly always asked, "what do you do for a living?"

As we explore how the idolatry of "what we do" may be present in our lives, we may become overwhelmed. We may react by thinking, "Ok, well, just tell me what to do." We may desire things to be simple and easy, but the realities of the heart are complex, and we have a *relationship* with God, not lists of "do this" and "don't do that." Dismantling the idols that have become lodged in our hearts takes time, and the impulse to "do" actually reveals a heart that has been shaped in a particular way. This can be part of the attraction of a religious system of *dos and don'ts*. It doesn't take faith or trust but simply the either/or of "doing." We're either in or we're out. We either did it or we didn't. This can be our thought process. While it is not gracious or lifegiving, it is manageable. However, God's heart for us is not to live a manageable life but a life flowing with goodness and grace that is rooted in relationship. Relationship can feel like a fuzzy word, perhaps even a bit vague. However, if we put it in terms of identity, we can ask: do you see yourself, as your core identity, as a beloved son or daughter of God?

It is interesting to note that before Jesus had *done* any work or accomplished any ministry, He was baptized (Matthew 3). At His baptism, He heard those words we discussed last week, "this is my beloved son in whom I am well pleased." Belovedness, relationship, and value do not come as a result of work but should be what lead us into the work/the "doing" of life. Then, of course, the next stop in Matthew 4 was the wilderness temptation where this was all challenged. In verses 8-9, we read: "Again, the devil took him to a very high mountain and showed him all the kingdoms of the world and their glory. And he said to him, 'All these I will give you, if you will fall down and worship me.'" In a very basic way, the temptation for Jesus was to "do" life on His own terms … to circumnavigate the suffering of the cross and go straight to being a king. His "doing" in life, we see over and over again, was shaped by a responsiveness to His Father. In John 5:19, Jesus says, "The Son can do nothing of His own accord but only what He sees the Father doing." Relationship, connection with the Father, was primary and foundational.

As we are pressed into a wilderness space where we are limited in what we can do and things are stripped away, our prayers can be shaped by wanting to get around the suffering or they can be shaped by resting in our identity as the beloved. The loss of a dream or the loss of ability to "do" can be a deep grace if we are willing to receive it that way. Rather than asking God to get us out of the desert, what would it be like to rest in *what is*? How might you receive *what is* as an invitation to press more deeply into your identity as one who is living in a relationship with God?

As we make that kind of choice, we begin to experience that His love is enough … that His presence is more satisfying than anything we might do or accomplish. We are able to say with confidence, "It is not about what I do, but who I am as a son (or daughter) of God." It is a life of resting in faith and trust rather than striving to accomplish. To be sure, this is not easy. It is upside down from what we have often experienced. Henri Nouwen said it so beautifully, "Jesus' [life] is characterized by a downward pull. That is what disturbs us. We cannot even think about ourselves in terms other than those of an upward pull, an upward mobility in which we strive for better lives, higher salaries and more prestigious positions. Thus, we are deeply disturbed by a God who embodies a downward movement."

As opposed to the false self which is about *what we do*, the true self is resting in our belovedness and actually letting God love us … receiving His presence as enough. What might that look like for you? How will you release an identity based on doing and remember that God is loving you, He is with you?

Notice the way Habakkuk describes resting in faith (the heart of true worship) in the following: "Though the fig tree should not blossom, nor fruit be on the vines, the produce of the olive fail and the fields yield no food, the flock be cut off from the fold and there be no herd in the stalls, yet I will rejoice in the LORD; I will take joy in the God of my salvation. GOD, the Lord, is my strength; he makes my feet like the deer's; he makes me tread on my high places." (3:17–19)

Question for reflection: how do you see the false self of "what we do" at work in your life?

Prayer: Lord, give me the strength to rest in relationship with You. Give me the wisdom to see You and listen to You in the ways you desire to be with me and love me. Amen.

Day 14 – What We Have

Not only does the false self show up as we are tempted to craft an identity around "what we do," it can also arise as we connect our hearts to "what we have." Certainly, in the wilderness, so often shaped by loss or lack, we are very aware of what we don't have. The idolatry of what we possess can be quite deceptive because what we possess are generally good things, needed things. The trouble arises in *how* we are possessing them.

As the wilderness lays us bare, we become aware that things are amiss and the need for deep soul work is brought to our attention. Our impulse can be to deal with it on our own, to use our own resources to address our emptiness, nakedness, and loneliness. The impulse "to do" or produce is a response to the emptiness (we explored this yesterday), the impulse to "possess" response to the experience of feeling naked, or exposed. Tomorrow, we will explore how we deal with our loneliness through the idol of "what other's think about us." All of these are self-protective strategies and time in the wilderness is designed to strip of these things so we will take up what God provides.

First, what are the specific possessions we may use to protect or cover ourselves? It could be so many things: finances, good health, family, nationality, knowledge, relationships, experiences, etc. Let's pause here for a moment. Do you use any of these "possessions" to cover your shame? Are there other "possessions" the Lord is bringing to your awareness? You might consider what it would be like to lose any of these things. What happens in your heart and mind as you reflect? Do you notice yourself in some kind of discomfort? Is there a reaction of clinging or grasping?

Dismantling the idol of "what we have" occurs as we notice our attachment and clinging, and then trust that God's provision is enough. Unexamined, our clinging to things other than Christ can function like a computer program running underneath our awareness. Advertisers and marketers know this incredibly well and utilize it to stir a "sense of need" where need does not necessarily exist. The supposed scarcity of things is also something that can cultivate an attachment to things, even a hoarding of possessions.

The challenge for us … do we believe that what God's provides is enough? Do we believe that life in in Him is truly abundant? And are we noticing when our hunger and need is being manipulated? For Jesus in the wilderness, the enemy came to Him to attempt to exploit the real hunger He was experiencing as He fasted. "'If you are the Son of God, command these stones to become loaves of bread.' But He answered, 'It is written, 'Man shall not live by bread alone but by every word that comes from the mouth of God.'" (Matthew 4:3-4) Notice how Jesus responds. He doesn't deny that He was hungry. He also doesn't deny that bread is something needed for life. He does refuse to trust in His own resources (as the Son of God) to cover His hunger. Finally, He also recognized that something deeper than physical hunger was in play: will I trust where the Father has me right now? Jesus' trust/rest in being the beloved was being tested, as is ours in a wilderness season.

Jesus's response of not living by bread alone is a quote from Deuteronomy 8:3 and in the verse that follows we find a fascinating statement: "Your clothing did not wear out on you and your foot did not swell these forty years." It might seem like a meaningless detail. However, the inclusion of this detail, right after talking about the provision of manna and that their lives were sustained by God, points to something deeper than just clothes and good foot health. God was saying, "I took care of you. I provided for you." As we consider how naked and exposed we feel in the wilderness, God wants to remind us of His provision. In 1 Peter 1:4, we read that in Christ, we have "an inheritance (clothing, provision) that is imperishable, undefiled, and unfading." And then, Peter discusses walking through trials so that our faith is tested. By faith, we trust in God's provision for all things we need, and then that faith is tested. The prayer of David in Psalm 23 reminds us of this perspective as well … "The Lord is my Shepherd; I don't need a thing."

1 John 2:16 calls this temptation to idolatry "pride in one's possessions," and it highlights the need for humility. David Benner echoes this: "The way of the true self is always the way of humility.

Pride and arrogance move us toward our false self, but humility and love allow us to live the truth of our being." As we become aware of our need being stirred and directed away from humble trust, we look to God in humility, trusting in His provision.

So, in contrast to the expression of the false self which is about *what we have*, the true self rests in God's provision … receiving His provision as enough. What might that look like for you? How will you release an identity based on possessions and remember that what He provides is truly enough?

Question for reflection: how do you see the false self of "what we have" at work in your life?

Prayer: Lord, give me the wisdom to see Your provision and to humbly trust that it is enough for me. I am grateful for the way that You provide everything I need for a life of godliness. Amen.

Day 15 – What Others Think of Us

In the wilderness spaces of life, one of the distinct features that can arise is loneliness. When suffering, the experience of aloneness can be quite profound. Our response can be either to resist and manage those difficult emotions with our own resources, or to discover how the Lord might desire to be with us in the loneliness and isolation. Loneliness and the feelings of alienation are common human experiences, and for many of us we learned how to navigate them at an early age. We learned how to do things to either get noticed by others or to stay off the radar that could lead to potential criticism. As we continue to consider idolatry, we can make an idol of what others think of us. It can be a place we go to receive what can only come from God.

Henri Nouwen described this clearly: "I am constantly surprised at how I keep taking the gifts God has given me - my health, my intellectual and emotional gifts - and keep using them to impress people, receive affirmation and praise, and compete for rewards, instead of developing them for the glory of God."

An awareness of this idol often shows up in the solitude of the desert because when we experience loneliness, there is no one to impress … there is no one to put salve in the wounds of loneliness. All the relational props and strategies get knocked away in the isolation of the wilderness. If it is a time of severe illness, we may lose the ability to seem strong or perhaps competent. If it is the suffering of broken relationship or a lost career, we may lose the sense that we are important. The gift in times like these is that we are left with nothing, just us. Just us and God. It may not feel like a gift … but what can emerge is the experience of being enough. Not only that God is enough, but that we are enough. We can stand on our own in Christ. We become deeply aware of our significance, giftedness, dignity, and value that transcends both the affirmation and denigration of others.

The people of Israel were collectively confronted with a sense of isolation and vulnerability. In Exodus 32:1, the text simply notes that *Moses delayed*. Packed into that word "delayed" is certainly a sense of loneliness and abandonment. Rather than seeking God in that moment, the people went to what was familiar. As Jesus journeyed through His forty days, the devil sought to exploit the loneliness and isolation of the desert as he tempted Jesus from the pinnacle of the temple with "If you are the Son of God, throw yourself down, for it is written, 'He will command his angels concerning you,' and 'On their hands they will bear you up, lest you strike your foot against a stone.'" (Matthew 4:6) The temptation was to put on a show, to perform … to deal with the isolation by using His relationship with the Father to do a miracle. Jesus simply responds with "You shall not put the Lord your God to the test." (v. 7) In other words, "I am not going to try to get God the Father to show up for me according to my perceived needs, but instead I will trust His love and plans for me." Jesus modeled rest as opposed to striving. He didn't need an outside source of validation.

Jesus also modeled this at the cross. In Hebrews 12:2, we read: "who for the joy that was set before him endured the cross, despising the shame, and is seated at the right hand of the throne of God." On the cross, Jesus hung battered, bruised, bleeding, and naked … executed as a criminal. The loneliness He experienced was excruciating, "My God, My God, why have you forsaken me?" (Psalm 22) The mocking, "if you are the Son of God, come down from the cross … save yourself" (Matt 27:40ff), was intense. The shame was quite palpable. Jesus *despised* (or, let go of) the shame because of the joy set before Him.

For Jesus, "the joy set before Him" was living into the fulfilment of everything that had been planned for Him. He could let go of the shame (and need to validate Himself) because of what had been promised and proclaimed about Him. For us, in a time of loneliness and isolation in the wilderness, we can also release the shame and trust in what God has said about us. We can let go of people pleasing strategies and rest in the reality that in Christ we are enough.

We may believe that the promise of an abundant life in Christ is true, and we also might be plagued with the idea that we aren't the kind of person who could live into the fullness of that life. For the people of Israel, God had promised them entry into a land where they could grow in love and faithfulness. He was also leading them into it. However, we know from Numbers 13:32-33 that they compared themselves to those already in the land and became afraid: "the land, through which we have gone to spy it out, is a land that devours its inhabitants, and all the people that we saw in it are of great height." Fear gripped them, and fear is often the companion of the loneliness and isolation of the wilderness. We just aren't so sure we have what it takes. From that place of insecurity, we can rely upon what others think to fill the gaps. We may try to fill the emptiness with the applause and approval of others.

As we reflect on this and then release the false self (of what others think about us), we can then remember that in Christ we are complete. The prayer of Ephesians 2:19 ("that you may be filled with the fullness of God") is a prayer that we would experience what is already true about us. See Colossians 2:9-10, "for in him the whole fullness of deity dwells bodily, and you have been filled in him."

Question for reflection: can you see ways that you try to please people or attempt to get people to think about you a certain way?

Prayer: Lord, I release this idol of defining myself based on what others think. Thank for you taking me into wilderness spaces where I am confronted with this. I desire to experience the reality that I am filled and complete in You. Amen.

Day 16 – Awake When the Sun Rises

Over the last week, we have examined the ways that idolatry might be present in our lives. Rather than understanding idolatry as the worship of something physical or external to ourselves, we have looked at the ways that idolatry is primarily an issue of the heart. Idolatry occurs as we rely upon things (including ourselves) to provide things that only God can provide. We were made for Him and we are His (Psalm 100). Idolatry is not merely a sin against God. It is a sin against ourselves and our created design.

In the wilderness, we are exposed. We experience an emptiness, nakedness, and vulnerability. Christ offers Himself to cover and protect us. This is why we read in Romans 15: "put on the Lord Jesus Christ, and make no provision for the flesh, to gratify its desires." In the desolation of wilderness, we become aware of all the old clothing that we put on to cover our nakedness and shame. We see more clearly and sense the invitation from God to: "put off your old self, which belongs to your former manner of life and is corrupt through deceitful desires … and put on the new self, created after the likeness of God in true righteousness and holiness." (Eph 4:22-24) A clothing metaphor is used here and in other portions of Scripture. Clothing serves a practical function – it covers and protects, and it also has an identification aspect – it signifies who we are. We generally choose to wear clothing that fits – both our body and our identity.

For Adam and Eve, when they became aware of their nakedness – they picked up fig leaves and began to hide – hiding not only their nakedness but hiding themselves from God. (cf. Genesis 3) The tragedy of the false self is that we think we're covering and protecting ourselves (and in a sense we are) but more than that we're hiding ourselves from God.

In so many ways, this is an unintended consequence. As we worship (give ourselves to) the gods of the false self, we are hiding from God because the attention of our heart and mind is on what we do, what we have, and what others think of us.

Over the centuries, there have been those who have intentionally inhabited a desert space. Commenting on the motivation, Belden Lane observed: "The desert monks were hardly naïve despisers of culture. What they fled with greatest fear was not the external world, but the world they carried inside themselves: an ego-centeredness needing constant approval, driven by compulsive behavior, frantic in its effort to attend to a self-image that always required mending." (*The Solace of Fierce Landscapes*)

As we choose to abide in the wilderness, even when our entry was not a choice, and intentionally remove the clothing of the false self, we pick up the clothing of God's presence, provision, and proclamation. He is our covering, our protection. Wilderness is, in this sense, a deep grace … a gift that we couldn't receive any other way. It is a gift that we could never imagine or even know how to ask for. The movement from *striving* (what the false self demands) to *rest* (what God offers in true self) is not something we achieve, possess, or earn. In fact, those are the strategies of the old clothing, the false self. This *rest* is something we receive as gift. It is something that we enter into as we are aware.

Thomas Merton offered a perspective on the wilderness that roots us in the gift that it truly is: "The Desert Fathers believed that the wilderness had been created as supremely valuable in the eyes of God precisely because it had no value to men. The wasteland was the land that could never be wasted by men because it offered them nothing. There was nothing to attract them. There was nothing to exploit. The desert was the region in which the Chosen People had wandered for forty years, cared for by God alone. They could have reached the Promised Land in a few months if they had travelled directly to it. God's plan was that they should learn to love Him in the wilderness and that they should always look back upon the time in the desert as the idyllic time of their life with Him alone."

Our task in the desert is to stay awake and alert in order to be aware of the invitations. An ancient story illustrates this beautifully. An apprentice asks his spiritual master about the value of spiritual practice. "What can I specifically do to reach enlightenment?" The master responded, "As but as much as you can do to make the sun rise." A bit perplexed, the disciple asks, "Then, why pray?" "Ah, so that you are awake when the sun rises?"

Ah, that we would be awake when the sun rises! That we would receive that awareness of His love and rest there in delight!

Consider these words from Psalm 37, "dwell in the land … and befriend faithfulness … delight yourself in the Lord … be still before the Lord … wait patiently for Him." Sit with those words for a few moments. What stands out to you? How is the Lord shaping your heart right now?

Question for reflection: how are you waking to the Lord's love and activity in your life?

Prayer: Lord, by Your mercy and through faith, may I be awake to Your love and the ways You are shaping me in this season. Give me the wisdom and courage to release the idols to which I tend to cling … that I might attach more fully to Your heart. Amen.

Third Sunday
Remember God's Goodness in the Previous Week

On Sundays, we are invited to pause in order to remember God's goodness and His work in us on the journey thus far. In Psalm 106, the history of Israel's time in the wilderness is recounted and it is said that they "forgot his works" (vs. 13) and "they forgot God" (vs. 21). Remembering is vital for abiding with God on the path of love.

Use the following to engage in a time of examen prayer:
- Begin by quieting your heart before God and simply taking a few deep, slow breaths as you remember that you are in God's presence.

- Review the week with gratitude. What is the Spirit bringing to your awareness?

- Notice the ways that God has been present to you in the previous week.

- What are you thankful for? What might God want you to see that you didn't previously notice? Perhaps a place to repent?

- Select a part of your reflection from the week to pray over.

- Pray for the coming week.

Write out a prayer of thanksgiving and celebration as you look back and look forward.

Week Four

From Isolation to Intimacy, v. 8

Day 17 – Numbers 25

As we explore the next account of Israel's time in the wilderness, we move a bit deeper into trust as we examine the issue of intimacy. The word intimacy itself elicits various emotions and thoughts. Perhaps fear and confusion or perhaps longing and anticipation. Maybe curiosity. No matter our initial response, may we grow in our responsive to the Lord's invitation to move from isolation to intimacy.

Once again, in the wilderness, the people of Israel struggled to trust God with their hearts … to follow Him in the dry, desolate desert. Specifically, Paul alludes to an episode from Numbers 25 as he challenges the Corinthian believers with: "we must not indulge in sexual immorality as some of them did, and twenty-three thousand fell in a single day." (1 Cor 10:8) Before looking at Numbers, it is helpful to understand that the religious climate of Corinth in the first century included worship of false gods that mixed worship and sexual expression. In Corinthian temples, worship which included sex with prostitutes was a temptation and was seducing followers of Christ.

In Numbers 25:1-3, we read that something very similar occurred with significant consequences: "While Israel lived in Shittim, the people began to whore with the daughters of Moab. These invited the people to the sacrifices of their gods, and the people ate and bowed down to their gods. So Israel yoked himself to Baal of Peor. And the anger of the LORD was kindled against Israel." The word "whore" in verse 1 and "yoked" in verse 3 speak to the sexual immorality that was occurring, and it was occurring in a religious context. The people were attaching themselves through ritual, sexualized worship of false gods.

Before you tune out and wonder about the relevance of a discussion like this, hang in there for a few more minutes. While there is much that could be said about the context and design for sexual activity in general, the specific context in both 1 Corinthians and Numbers is worth noting. What is being addressed is the mixture of sexuality with worship. Again, you may wonder about the relevance. Certainly, in today's world, we don't seem to be tempted in quite this same way.

However, the connection with worship might actually be pointing to something more significant about sexuality than we might perceive at first blush. In fact, understanding the link with worship might open our eyes to the beauty and gift of sexuality in transformative ways.

If we look at the broader context in 1 Corinthians, we see that a discussion of sexuality is laced throughout the pages of the letter. In particular, 1 Corinthians 6:13-20 uses the phrase *sexual immorality* (as in 10:8) several times and also draws some helpful distinctions that can help us see the relevance to our lives:

> *"Food is meant for the stomach and the stomach for food'—and God will destroy both one and the other. The body is not meant for sexual immorality, but for the Lord, and the Lord for the body. And God raised the Lord and will also raise us up by his power. Do you not know that your bodies are members of Christ? Shall I then take the members of Christ and make them members of a prostitute? Never! Or do you not know that he who is joined to a prostitute becomes one body with her? For, as it is written, 'The two will become one flesh.' But he who is joined to the Lord becomes one spirit with him. Flee from sexual immorality. Every other sin a person commits is outside the body, but the sexually immoral person sins against his own body. Or do you not know that your body is a temple of the Holy Spirit within you, whom you have from God? You are not your own, for you were bought with a price. So glorify God in your body."*

Note the statement: "food is meant for the stomach and the stomach for food." This was a common saying in that first century context, and a metaphor for saying "It's a natural function of the body to engage in sexual activity." The response was not to say that sex is unnatural or not a part of our design, but that we need to direct our gaze a bit higher. Our bodies and sexuality have to be understood in the context of our relationship with God. Specifically, our body is designed to be enjoyed and experienced "for the Lord." Even more specifically, our body is a temple (a dwelling place) of the Holy Spirit. Our body is a place designed to glorify God.

To glorify something is to extol its essence. To glorify God is to bring honor to who He is. Another way we might say it is that to glorify God is to reflect His image, His essence. Our bodies were made to reflect His essence, and, of course, there are so many things we could say about the essence of God but perhaps the most relevant in this context is the connectedness of God. God, existing in three persons – Father, Son, and Holy Spirit, lives in eternal relationship and connection. This is why we can say that God is love. (1 John 4:8) What all of this points to is that perhaps the most significant way to glorify God is to experience a connectedness in our bodies. The immorality of the ancient people of Israel is that they were connecting/attaching with false gods. God desires that we connect with Him.

In the wilderness, as we look for comfort, love, and connection because of the disconnection and isolation we feel, the temptation is to look toward sex to dispel the disconnectedness. However, immorality results because this reverses the order of divine and human relationships. The sexualized worship of these Biblical passages presents a pattern which is all too common in our world today: use sex to attempt to find intimacy and ultimately become connected to something other than God. The divine pattern is finding intimacy, love, and connection with God which becomes the context for all other relational connections with others. When our experience of love is rightly ordered, sexuality (and really any relational connection) is a beautiful gift that points us back to the love of God and is also an expression of God's love.

So, our exploration this week is an invitation to search our hearts … to examine our feelings of disconnection and isolation and also to consider how intimacy finds its fullest realization. How do we bond with God in ways that are a fulfillment of our created design?

Questions for reflection: what is standing out to you in this movement from isolation to intimacy? Are you noticing any resistance to exploring the issue of intimacy?

Prayer: Lord, I acknowledge the messiness and confusion that often surrounds sexuality. Give me ears to hear what You desire to say to me this week and provide deepening insight into the ways that my body can connect with You. Amen.

Day 18 – Attaching to God

When we encounter deep longing for connection and love, we need discernment … especially as it relates to the sexual temptation which can be present. We need to be able to understand the processes and patterns that shape us and direct our thoughts and behavior. In addition, our discernment needs to be grounded in an experiential relationship with God. In his book, *Discernment,* Henri J.M. Nouwen offered: "God has created you and me with a heart that only God's love can satisfy. And every other love will be partial, will be real, but limited, will be painful. And if we are willing to let the pain prune us, to give us a deeper sense of our belovedness, then we can be as free as Jesus and walk on this world and proclaim God's first love, wherever we go."

In most of our communities of faith, we are familiar and comfortable with the *idea* that we are in a relationship with God. And we are likely not resistant to the *idea* that God loves us. However, we may have little to no experience actually encountering the love of God as more than an idea or theological truth. The love of God contains implications, in terms of truth and ideas, that are incredibly compelling and even helpful for framing things and developing an understanding of God and our lives. At the same time, the love of God is something to be experienced in such a way that we don't just say "God's loves me, this I know," but "yesterday, God loved me as I sensed His presence during my time with a friend" or "God said that He loved me this morning in my time of listening prayer" or "I didn't know what to say in a meeting yesterday. I paused and listened and heard a still small voice reminding me of something." When we are experiencing God in an interactive way, His love becomes a part of our lives in more ways than simply a *truth* perspective.

When we are experiencing and listening to God throughout our day, we are being transformed by His love. The primary word in the Hebrew scriptures for love is the word *hesed* which speaks of loyalty and connection. In Psalm 103 and 117, we read a description of this *hesed*: "great is His steadfast love toward us." The word *great* is a word that means "powerful" and is often translated "prevail." The idea is that His love is not just a powerful idea but has a real, shaping power in our lives. How exactly does this work?

We are shaped by our attachments. As we understand God's love as an attachment kind of love, we can rightly assert that His love is powerful. In his book *Renovated*, Jim Wilder writes: "in the human brain, identity and character are formed by who we love. Attachments are powerful and long lasting. Ideas can be changed more easily. Salvation through a new, lasting attachment to God that changes our identities would be a very relational way to understand our salvation: we [are) both saved and transformed through attachment love from, to, and with God." What is being highlighted, with the help of neuroscience, is that we are brought into a relationship and held in that relationship because God has attached Himself to us. Then, as we actually live in that relationship, we are being loved by God and becoming attached to Him.

This is why Paul was so concerned about sexual immorality. The relational processes that create bonding and attachment are enhanced significantly by the sexual experience. Chemicals that wash over our brain as a result of sex supercharge the bonding process. And that is a good thing – a gift from God. However, when that bonding process is mixed with false beliefs/false gods, it can wreak havoc. And, if the bonding process occurring in sex is ripped apart by casual sex or not in the context of a covenant relationship, it does damage to our attachment capacity. Trauma, addiction, and other kinds of relational hurt can affect our capacity as well.

In the coming days, we will explore more about finding healing and restoration where damage has occurred. For now, let's stay with the reality of God's attachment love toward us. In Psalm 63:1, 3, David wrote: "O God, you are my God; earnestly I seek you; my soul thirsts for you; my flesh faints for you, as in a dry and weary land where there is no water. Because your steadfast love is better than life, my lips will praise you." There is a connection between our longings and steadfast love (*hesed*) being better than life. Do you see an experiential connection to His love in your life? Not, do you believe this? But, are you experiencing this? Sit with this reality and this question for a few moments. What do you notice? What is God bringing to your awareness? How is God shaping your understanding of His love? What practical implications are you noticing?

As you experience a longing for connection, it is important to discern several things. First, it is helpful to discern and distinguish when we experience this kind of longing that only God can fully meet … so that we can name it and not just respond mechanically. Second, what are the ways that you tend to respond to the longing for connection and attachment? What might it be like to develop a habit and pattern of bringing those longings into a prayerful awareness with God?

In this context, Henri Nouwen shared: "The real work of prayer is to become silent and listen to the voice that says good things about me. To gently push aside and silence the many voices that question my goodness and to trust that I will hear the voice of blessing - that demands real effort." Take a few moments and ask God to bring your longing for connection and attachment to your awareness. What questioning voices come to your awareness? Gently let them go and stay present to how God wants to connect with you. Notice His voice and presence with you.

Being established and renewed in the love of God does not happen overnight, but through consistent, patterned response to our longings for connection. Then, God becomes our all and the foundation from which we encounter all other relationships.

Question for reflection: how is God speaking to you? If you haven't already, sit further with the questions above.

Prayer: Lord, I desire to know Your love – not just intellectually but in my bones. I desire for You to be the one to whom I am attached before all others. May all other relationships flow from the love I experience with you. Amen.

Day 19 – Healing and Our Capacity to Love

Certainly, the people of Israel had been traumatized during their 400 years of slavery in Egypt. Their capacity to trust and receive the love of God was altered and diminished on some level. We've seen this portrayed in these last weeks as they struggled to receive all that God was providing. From their struggle to receive God's care (with the manna) to the timing of His provision (Moses' delay) to the misdirected desires for connection, they didn't fully know how to receive the love of God. The journey in the wilderness … feeling alone and abandoned and disconnected … was being used by God to draw them to His heart. The wilderness is a place of healing … of finding God to be our everything. However, it is a process. Transformation is not overnight.

Thomas Merton, in *Thoughts in Solitude,* highlights this: "The desert was created simply to be itself, not to be transformed by men into something else … the desert is therefore the logical dwelling place for the man who seeks to be nothing but himself--that is to say, a creature solitary and poor and dependent upon no one but God, with no great project standing between himself and his Creator." So, this leaves us with the question, is that what you seek? Pause here for a moment. Are you seeking to be nothing but dependent upon God? Are you desiring for the wilderness to strip you of your learned responses to life so you might experience a "reshaping" of your capacity to love and be loved?

There may be a level of desire in which we just want to numb our capacity … to get some relief. This is likely what was going on with the people of Israel in Numbers 25. Sex is often used this way. God's heart is that we find His love to be enough, but that can mean that we experience a bit of pain along the way as old relational strategies are laid bare so that new ones can emerge. It will likely mean letting go of some old strategies, involving some starts and stops along the way.

We are designed for intimacy … to love and be loved … to know and be known. Our design includes a beautiful capacity to attach to others in love. Attachment love (*hesed*) is God's love (*agape* in the New Testament), and it transforms us. It shapes us. This capacity is seen in the young child who looks to her parents to see how to respond to falling while trying to walk across the room. A seasoned married couple begins to know what the other is thinking without a word. In 2 Corinthians 5:14–15, we read about this kind of love: "For the love of Christ controls us, because we have concluded this: that one has died for all, therefore all have died; and he died for all, that those who live might no longer live for themselves but for him who for their sake died and was raised." The word "controls" is a Greek word (*sunexo*), meaning to hold together or hold fast. His love "controls" us in that it attaches to us – we experience a bonding with Him.

When we are aware that our capacity to know and be known has been diminished in some way (and this is true for all of us – to varying degrees), we are ready to experience the inner healing and formation that comes through the presence of Holy Spirit in our lives. Our woundedness could be from trauma, addictions, or other sufferings brought into our lives either because of harsh things that have happened or nurturing things that didn't happen.

As we intentionally hold fast to the One who holds us fast (i.e., look to Him), we experience this love. However, we often spend much of our lives unaware and nonattentive to His love in practical ways … letting that love touch the actual circumstances of our lives. Awareness and attentiveness begin most effectively as we integrate God's presence and activity into our story. Much as the child looks to the parent's eyes, we look to the eyes of the one who loves us more than we can imagine.

How does this work?

We begin with looking at those places of pain that we are tempted to numb or forget. In a wilderness season, by His grace, we are often more aware of these places than at other times. This is a grace even though it usually does not feel like it. We know from trauma research that trauma and pain often get stuck in our body and inhibit the ability to receive love. The "stuckness" happens when we are not able to process the pain the way our brains are wired to process and make sense of life … through integrating the events of life into our story. As children (sons and daughters) of God, we need to look into the eyes of God to see how our experiences (especially those painful ones) fit into His story … the larger story of life. Our small stories generally struggle to hold and give context for deep pain. So, as we bring our pain and hurts to God, our capacity to receive love finds healing and restoration. To put it simply, His story is the reality of His presence and work in our world to connect with His creation through Jesus.

So, we start with awareness. From this place of awareness, we move into attentiveness as we engage in a process of talking to God … asking the questions: *how were You present with me in this part of my life? God? What do You want me to see and understand about this part of my story?* Then, we listen … seeking to be attentive to what God brings to our hearts and minds. It can be helpful to write things down. As we become present to God's heart (what He says to us), we respond with gratefulness. In the great prayer book of the Bible (the Psalms), we see the people of God rehearsing their stories in the presence of God (integrating their experiences into His story) and the response is gratefulness and praise.

Question for reflection: is there an experience from the last day or week, or perhaps further back which God brings to your awareness? Take a few moments to sit with it and walk it through this process of integrating it into His story.

Prayer: Father, may I look into your eyes the ways a child looks to a parent to know what to think and how to respond. I desire to attach myself to You in love. Thank you for attaching Yourself to me. Amen.

Day 20 – Voices that Confuse & Hearing God's Voice

As we experience healing in those places where we have been hurt and traumatized, we are able to move into deepening intimacy with God. But even in our healing, one of the ongoing features of the journey is that we stumble and fall along the way. The people of Israel in the wilderness definitely display this reality. When we trip along the way (failing to respond to God's presence and the way He is leading us), we can retreat and isolate or it can become a place for intimacy and growth.

In the wilderness, the experience of isolation and loneliness is an invitation to intimacy. In Christ, we have an intimacy and closeness to God that is already in our possession. 1 Cor 2:16 tells us that "we have the mind of Christ." Indeed, it is our inheritance, and yet we often do not move toward that intimacy because of the patterns of isolation we may embrace as a response to our own sin. In the messiness of the desert, our sin and our brokenness are often more apparent and our strategies to distract, hide, or deny are not as available. So, we may isolate and retreat from God in order to go it alone. This, in turn, may lead to further independence in thought, choice, and action. From there, feelings of failure can lead to further isolation … creating a vicious cycle. The voices and questions we often hear in these spaces are: *get it together; everyone else seems to be doing just fine; what's wrong with you?; do you even love God?* The space of isolation can feel like too much to bear so we seek to find intimacy and love in things that can't meet the need.

This can be our pattern and yet God invites us to turn our gaze to Him, to look into His eyes, and perceive His heart … to experience His love. We may have misconceptions about how to approach God or even our worthiness to do so. Because we've been shaped by relationships in which we have perceived the need to measure up, perform, or please, we may have transferred these perceptions on to God. In their book *When Prayer Becomes Real,* John Coe and Kyle Stobel make the observation that "prayer is not a place to be good, but a place to be honest." God knows where we are, what we've done or left undone, and how we are thinking about things. He is not intimidated, repulsed, or any other response that is anything but love. Because of this, we not only can come to Him as we are but we should! Psalm 145:18 reminds us that "The Lord is near to all who call on Him." Of course, He is always near and always present but our experience of Him as near and our movement toward intimacy only occurs as we turn to Him, call on Him, and seek to look into His eyes. *Lord, what do you see? What are you noticing?*

The challenge of living in a place of isolation and independence is that we are left with our own thoughts and perceptions. Isaiah 55:8 describes the isolated soul: "for my thoughts are not your thoughts." Intimacy is to know and be known. The invitation to intimacy is to share and express where we are, and then to listen to God's heart about where we are. This could seem like a scary proposition, and numbing ourselves or trying to escape the desert may sound safer. The truth is that God does respond in love, He is for us, "there is nothing that can separate us from His love." (Romans 8:39) Pause here for a moment. Can you believe this about God? Can you believe it? It is incredible. There is nothing (not even my sin) that separates me from His love. We can go even a step further and say that – our sin – can be a connecting point to His love, a place to experience His love. What would it be like, if rather than isolating and going it alone with your sin, you stopped and went to Him?

"If we confess our sins," we experience the reality that He is faithful in grace toward us. (1 John 1:9) The word confess is a word that means "to say the same thing as" or to share the mind of another. Confess is an *intimacy word*. How do we say the same thing as God? We listen to Him. The invitation in confession is not to merely say "I know what I did or didn't do is wrong" but to listen to what God has to say about it – to share in His thoughts. If His approach toward us is in fact love, then He doesn't beat us over the head with our sin but gives us His wisdom and His insight. He shepherds us. He tenderly walks us forward and holds us close. An intimacy with God like this begins to shape us away from sin and isolation.

Intimacy is about conversation, talking to God about anything and everything … sharing our hearts with Him and asking Him what He sees and what He hears in our lives. We also ask: *God, how are you loving me God in this moment? How are you with me?* As every day, real things from our lives are touched by the love of God, His love moves from the theology book into our hearts and minds. Things like sexual immorality are no longer the temptation they once were because His love becomes more powerful. Sexual immorality, or other forms of immorality, are pursued because we have a lack of intimacy. But this a burden that is too heavy for sex, or any other created thing, to carry. The design is for us to experience a depth of love with God that can then give meaning to every part of our life.

Question for reflection: what might shift in the way you interact God? If you haven't already, pause for a few moments and talk to God about the first thing that comes to you mind. Then, ask Him what He sees and hears in what you are experiencing.

Prayer: Lord, thank you for giving me the mind of Christ so that I might know your thoughts and perspectives on all that I experience. May I draw to close to your heart and listen in all the circumstances of my life. I desire the intimacy that you offer. Amen.

Day 21 – Gentleness Amidst the Harsh

Wilderness seasons are harsh … a dry and weary land that can leave us feeling beat up, bruised, and thirsty. The wilderness can lead us to wonder if anyone cares. It may seem easy to stay on the path when there is a cool breeze and green grass next to us on the path along a beautiful ocean. However, when we feel like we are the only ones who are continuing on the path in the wilderness season, the solitariness of it all can really take a toll. Then, the despair may feel a bit thicker when we see others experience a depth of pain that comes from the consequences of their sin.

After the incident with the sexualized worship in Moab, significant consequences came to those who engaged in this sin. We read: "And the LORD said to Moses, 'Take all the chiefs of the people and hang them in the sun before the LORD, that the fierce anger of the LORD may turn away from Israel.' And Moses said to the judges of Israel, 'Each of you kill those of his men who have yoked themselves to Baal of Peor.'" (Numbers 25:4–5) The harshness of this consequence baffles the mind. There is a gravity and sadness as we consider it. It can feel like there is no hope in the dusty, death-filled landscape of the wilderness.

Our longings for love and comfort are exposed even more in these days. In the wilderness, we desire so desperately to hear that it is going to be ok. And not just a glib pat on the shoulder but a gritty kind of presence that is with us in it. The kind of presence that speaks tenderly with tears in the eyes and pain in the voice. We want to know that we are not alone. We need to know that we are cared for. Is it worth it? Is this going somewhere?

As we allow ourselves to be present to the quietness of desolation, we may hear the quiet words "I will never leave you or forsake you." These words bounce around our soul and we may begin to notice some hope bubble to the surface. In this space, we start to become aware that the wilderness is not a problem to solve or an environment to master and control. In the releasing, we begin to see that there are streams of water imperceptible to the human eye … streams of life and hope and joy and peace.

God employs such imagery through the prophet Isaiah: "The wilderness and the dry land shall be glad; the desert shall rejoice and blossom like the crocus; it shall blossom abundantly and rejoice with joy and singing … for waters break forth in the wilderness, and streams in the desert; the burning sand shall become a pool, and the thirsty ground springs of water; in the haunt of jackals, where they lie down, the grass shall become reeds and rushes." (35:1-2, 6-7) Seeing this truth of what God does in the desert breathes freedom into our spirit. Instead of the wilderness being another prison, our imagination is enlivened to see that the desert is a space where God redeems and transforms and heals. As we begin to see, we begin to live. We begin to lose a preoccupation with self and with producing our own sense of comfort. We taste the "glorious freedom of the children of God." (Romans 8:21) The apostle Paul speaks of this freedom in the context of suffering and he also puts it in terms of the "groaning in the pains of childbirth." (8:22) Indeed, there is a great hope in the days of pregnancy, even in the pain, because of what is coming. But what if the pregnant woman didn't know she was pregnant? It would seem to be pain for no reason.

Michael Card, in his song *In the Wilderness*, sings: "Groaning and growing, amidst the desert days, the windy winter wilderness, can blow the self away." In the wilderness, the birthing process is marked by subtraction as the false self is shed. The pain of the pregnant wilderness is not something to numb but an invitation to hope and anticipation. It is in these moments that the tenderness of God's love becomes quite real. One of the elements of an intimate relationship that emerge during the birthing process is the ritual of *naming*. A name is selected that represents hopes and desires. God does the same with us. In Revelation 2:12-17, we find a letter written to a church that was dealing the same things as the people of Israel in Numbers 25. (note the references to Balak and Balaam as in Numbers 24). God shares that He gives to those who overcome (i.e., stay on the path) "a white stone with a new name written on it." (Rev 2:17)

Spend a few moments with the One who will never leave you or forsake you. Pray a simple prayer: *Lord, what is Your name for me?* Listen and receive what the Lord has for you in this season.

Questions for reflection: what is the name on that white stone? What does that name communicate to you? How does it enliven hope?

Prayer: Lord, here I am, dry and thirsty – desiring You more than anything else, trusting that You are with me and at work in me. Give me eyes to see what You see, and ears to hear what You hear that I might perceive that stream in the wilderness. Amen.

Day 22 – Embracing Silence to Draw Close

As we have examined the admonition about sexual immorality, you may have noticed that we have not dissected the issue of sexual immorality but have instead looked at the issue of intimacy and locating our desire for intimacy in the context of our life with God. While there may be other factors in play, sexual immorality is primarily an intimacy issue. At the end of the day, sexual immorality is not the problem … it is *a perceived* solution employed to deal with an intimacy problem.

When we experience isolation and loneliness, our needs and desires for intimacy come to the foreground of awareness. The invitation in loneliness is to remember that you are not alone. In the repentance pattern of reflect, release, and remember, we reflect on the experience of feeling alone or lonely, we release strategies to meet those needs on our own terms, and then remember that we are not truly alone. This is simple but not easy, especially if we have developed and habituated strategies from decades of life experience. As we reflect, we have to feel the loneliness and stick with it … seeking God in it in order to meet Him there and let Him love us and reassure us. As we do this, we are developing an orientation of listening to His voice as the way we interact with the loneliness and isolation of a wilderness season.

Dietrich Bonhoeffer, in his classic *Life Together,* offers this counsel: "Let him who cannot be alone beware of community. Let him who is not in community beware of being alone." This describes the push and pull of loving God and loving others. The greatest commandment, which is to love, contains both the love of God and love of neighbor for this reason. We can't love others unless rooted in and fueled by a loving relationship with God. Without this grounding, we will likely experience significant unhealth in relationships because we will need people to be who they can never be … asking them to provide what only God can. On the other hand, as we grow in our comfort with and commitment to being alone with God, the love we experience needs to be expressed and poured out to others.

We have a tendency in difficult relational seasons to scan the landscape and imagine the worst … to feel overwhelmed. For the people of Israel as they were leaving Egypt, Pharoah and his army came against them at the edge of the Red Sea. Observe their reaction: "the people of Israel cried out to the Lord. They said to Moses, 'Is it because there are no graves in Egypt that you have taken us away into the wilderness to die? What have you done to us?'" (Exodus 14:11) When confronted with challenging human relationships, we often respond with some variation of "I'm going to die … this is just too much for me." Notice Moses' response: "Fear not, stand firm, and see the salvation of the Lord, which he will work for you today. For the Egyptians whom you see today, you shall never see again. The Lord will fight for you, and you have only to be silent." (v.13-14)

Moses clearly names what can happen to us in relational wilderness seasons: fear. The encouragement is to look into the eyes of God … to see Him in all His glory. He affirms that the Lord is present with them and they don't have to run. The only thing required: be silent. Incorporating silence into our regular rhythms is a gift that we learn to appreciate in the wilderness. David Vryhof, SSJE, reflects on this: "Seek the gifts that come from time with God alone. Develop the inner quality of solitude of heart. Learn to abide in the hermitage within. Love your cell. 'The cell will teach you all things.'" One of the desert fathers commented that if we discipline ourselves to spend time in our prayer cell, we can begin to take our prayer cells with us. This is the pattern that Jesus modeled for us: embracing silence in order to draw close.

For Jesus, there were times when the demands of the crowd became incredibly significant. In Mark 1:33, we read that "the whole city gathered together at the door." The next "morning, while it was still dark, he departed and went out to a desolate place, and there he prayed." (v. 35) We see this pattern in Jesus over and over again. He would withdraw to quiet and solitude so that He could then return to be close to others … to engage with them, teach them, heal them, love them. This was not always understood by those around Him. In the following verses, the account suggests that the disciples searched for him and in bewilderment said, "Everyone is looking for you."

Living into the fullness of human relationships without demanding more than they can offer and also not letting them demand more than you can offer necessitates that we embrace an intentional rhythm of retreat and engagement.

What might that look like for you? The rhythm of retreat/engage can be a gift in moments when a simple ten-minute retreat with God could offer the needed centering in various relational circumstances. And certainly, a larger rhythm of retreat is a vital aspect of relational, spiritual, physical, and emotional health.

Questions for reflection: sit quietly with what we have considered this week. What stands out to you? What has resonated? What is the invitation you are sensing?

Prayer: Lord, I confess that You are what my heart desires. Thank You for Your grace in meeting me again and again and inviting me to connect with Your heart and look into Your eyes for what I most need. Amen.

Fourth Sunday
Remember God's Goodness in the Previous Week

On Sundays, we are invited to pause in order to remember God's goodness and His work in us on the journey thus far. In Psalm 106, the history of Israel's time in the wilderness is recounted and it is said that they "forgot his works" (vs. 13) and "they forgot God" (vs. 21). Remembering is vital for abiding with God on the path of love.

Use the following to engage in a time of examen prayer:
- Begin by quieting your heart before God and simply taking a few deep, slow breaths as you remember that you are in God's presence.

- Review the week with gratitude. What is the Spirit bringing to your awareness?

- Notice the ways that God has been present to you in the previous week.

- What are you thankful for? What might God want you to see that you didn't previously notice? Perhaps a place to repent?

- Select a part of your reflection from the week to pray over.

- Pray for the coming week.

Write out a prayer of thanksgiving and celebration as you look back and look forward.

Week Five

From Certainty to Humility, v.9

Day 23 – The Temptation of Certainty

A common phrase often heard among churches and people of faith is: "God showed up." This is uttered when something inspiring or seemingly miraculous happens, or it is heard in prayers: "God, we really need you to show up." The idea of "God showing up" was also a feature in one of the temptations Jesus encountered in Matthew 4. The enemy challenged Jesus to throw Himself off the temple because "He *(God)* will command His angels concerning" which is a quote from Psalm 91. Jesus resolutely responded with "you shall not put the Lord your God to the test." (Deuteronomy 6:16)

So, how was this about testing God? Essentially, the devil suggested that Jesus could demand from God the Father … that He could expect Him to "show up" in a certain way. This was testing God in the sense that it took something known about God from the Scriptures and presumed that God would necessarily be present in that way. Presumption is dangerous because it assumes that we know what God will do, when He will do it, or how He will do it. Oswald Chambers teased out this issue: "Have you been asking God what He is going to do? He will never tell you! God does not tell you what He is going to do; He reveals to you who He is."

We can only know *the who of God*, not the what, when, or how. The phrase "God showed up" puts us in dangerous territory because we presume to know the *what, when, or how*. In addition, the phrase is most often used to describe good or favorable things that have happened. It is not generally used to talk about God's presence with us in difficulties or His presence with us when He seems silent. The presumption is we can expect God to bring about good or favorable things. The problem is that usually our definitions of good or favorable are not the whole picture. The assumption in "God showed up" is that God is present only at certain times and in certain ways. Yet, He is always with us and always loving us.

In a wilderness season, when there is so much we just don't know and even things that are confusing, we need a sense of security. Rather than finding security in who God is, we often reach for it in certainty … desiring some certainty as to what God will do and how

He will do it. We see the danger of pursuing certainty in 1 Corinthians 10:9 as Paul warns: "We must not put Christ to the test, as some of them did and were destroyed by serpents." The incident with serpents is found in Numbers 21:4–6: "From Mount Hor they set out by the way to the Red Sea, to go around the land of Edom. And the people became impatient on the way. And the people spoke against God and against Moses, 'Why have you brought us up out of Egypt to die in the wilderness? For there is no food and no water, and we loathe this worthless food.' Then the LORD sent fiery serpents among the people, and they bit the people, so that many people of Israel died." This question about being brought to the wilderness to die surfaces again, and God disciplined them with the serpents in order to wake them up. And in fact, they did wake up and confess they had spoken against God. This is described as testing God because they were presuming that God would and should show up in certain ways.

Ironically, this complaint occurred just after God had given them victory over a Canaanite king who had attacked and captured some of the people of Israel. Clearly, He was with them and was involved in protecting them. But, it can be a temptation to presume that because God acted in a particular way in one situation that He will do it again. Specifically, we may transfer what we know about God, His attributes and character, onto what we don't know with certainty about God, which is a lot. Of course, we have all the knowledge we need to love and trust God, but sometimes we can be tempted to think that it is not enough. We want to know *what, when, and how*, and either presume He will be present in certain ways or that He should have been present in certain ways. A life of faith is not about certainty but trust – specifically, trusting a person. When certainty is the pursuit, we interact with God based on what we want to be true rather than what is. It is not true that God heals every sickness or protects us from every danger in life. What is true is that He is good, He love us, He is holy, and the list could go on.

Finally, in Exodus 17:7 we read: "And he called the name of the place Massah and Meribah, because of the quarreling of the people of Israel, and because they tested the LORD by saying, 'Is the LORD among us or not?'" This question reveals a heart that is both not trusting and not humble. In a reference to this account in Exodus, we read in the prayer of Psalm 95:7-9: "Today, if you hear his voice, do not harden your hearts, as at Meribah, as on the day at Massah in the wilderness, when your fathers put me to the test and put me to the proof, though they had seen my work." God graciously calls us to listen to Him moment by moment and this puts us in a place of trust. If we pursue certainty, we are seeking (perhaps unintentionally) to be without a need to trust. Trust leaves us in a place of vulnerability and need, and if we could have certainty, we would have no need of God.

Certainty, the *what, how, and when* of life is an illusion. This week, we explore the movement from certainty to humility. Humility rises when we lay down our pursuit of certainty and what we believe we can know about God. Surviving in the wilderness is not about God showing up but us showing up. God is always present and our invitation is to keep our hearts open to Him rather than having a hardened heart shaped by presumption and expectation. We "show up" with humility, knowing and embracing our vulnerability and need.

Questions for reflection: when are you tempted to seek certainty? In what ways is the Lord is speaking to your heart today?

Prayer: Lord, I come to You with a heart that is open. Give me wisdom to see places where I presume upon You, and may I move toward humility. Amen.

Day 24 – Doubt: A Friend of Faith

When we experience doubt, it can throw us. It can come unexpectedly, and it may provoke a sense of shame or discouragement. Our doubt can spiral into more doubt. The desert seasons are often filled with doubt as we wonder if we will make it, we wonder if God is really good, we wonder why this is all happening. Our impulse may be to try to get rid of the doubt but that can be the worst idea. Because there are so many things for which we can't be certain, doubt is a sign that we are paying attention. If we never have doubts, perhaps we are not living by faith but presumption or even arrogance.

Doubt is actually a friend of faith. When we experience doubt, it is an invitation to trust … to place my faith in who I know God to be. To be sure, doubt often leads to a purification and clarification of what we know and trust. This can be a process and a bit of a journey, but this is part of what God graciously does in the wilderness. We are stripped of preconceived ideas and presumption. We are left with a simplicity that is incredibly profound. It is not without frustration and even pain but can also lead to deep joy and a peace that surpasses understanding … if we let it.

In Exodus 17, the people asked the question … "is God among us or not?" There was doubt. They wondered. Their question was not a bad question in and of itself. It was their interaction with the question that led them astray into grumbling, quarreling, and testing God. However, it could have led them to a deeper experience of trust. A movement toward humility is essential as we encounter doubt.

Once again, if we are paying attention, there is an uncertainty that hangs over life. We do not know what tomorrow may bring. (Proverbs 27:1) This is echoed in the wisdom of James: "Come now, you who say, 'Today or tomorrow we will go into such and such a town and spend a year there and trade and make a profit'— yet you do not know what tomorrow will bring. What is your life? For you are a mist that appears for a little time and then vanishes. Instead, you ought to say, 'If the Lord wills, we will live and do this or that.' As it is, you boast in your arrogance. All such boasting is evil." (4:13–16) As we release "knowing" and embrace humility, we are freed to be able to listen to God in the present moment. Being present to God and responding to His voice (cf., Psalm 95:7-9) is the essence of a humble faith. An insistence on knowing can lead to a hardened heart in which we can't see God and perceive His presence with us.

Anthony DeMello developed this idea quite profoundly: "The fact is that you are surrounded by God and yet you don't see God, because you 'know' about Him. The final barrier to the vision of God is our God concept. You miss God because you think you know. That's the terrible thing about religion. That's what the Gospels were saying – that religious people 'knew,' so they got rid of Jesus. The highest knowledge of God is to know God as unknowable." It may sound confusing to think of God as unknowable. There are clearly things we can know of God, but this highlights the mystery involved in following Jesus. Humility in faith requires that we exercise the repentance rhythm of reflect, release, remember. We reflect on the potential presence of presumption and quest for certainty in our lives, we release, and then remember that we are finite, limited creatures who are dependent upon the infinite God of the universe.

Jesus also spoke boldly about the issue of "knowing" to the religious leaders of His day: "Jesus said, 'For judgment I came into this world, that those who do not see may see, and those who see may become blind.' Some of the Pharisees near him heard these things, and said to him, 'Are we also blind?' Jesus said to them, 'If you were blind, you would have no guilt; but now that you say, "We see," your guilt remains.'" (John 9:39–41) For us to embrace "blindness" is the epitome of humility. While we may find it a bit discouraging or even disorienting to release "knowing" in a presumptuous way, we can move further into trust. Consider the words of the Apostle Paul in 2 Corinthians 4:16-18: "So we do not lose heart. Though our outer self is wasting away, our inner self is being renewed day by day. For this light momentary affliction is preparing for us an eternal weight of glory beyond all comparison, as we look not to the things that are seen but to the things that are unseen. For the things that are seen are transient, but the things that are unseen are eternal."

Pause here for just a moment ... what do you notice the Spirit stirring in you? Pause to reflect, and then walk through the prayer below from John Baillie:

"Almighty and eternal God, You are hidden from my sight; You are beyond the understanding of my mind; Your thoughts are not as my thoughts; Your ways are past finding out. Yet You have breathed Your Spirit into my life; Yet You have formed my mind to seek You; Yet You have inclined my heart to love You; Yet You have made me restless for the rest that is in You; Yet You have planted within me a hunger and thirst that make me dissatisfied with all the joys of earth. O You who alone knows what lies before me this day, grant that in every hour of it I may stay close to You. Let me be in the world, yet not of it. Let me use this world without abusing it. If I buy, let me be as though I possessed not. If I have nothing, let me be as though possessing all things. Let me today embark on no undertaking that is not in line with You will for my life, nor shrink from any sacrifice Your will may demand. Suggest, direct, control every movement of my mind for my Lord Christ's sake. Amen."

Questions for reflection: as you consider a wilderness season in your own life, are there doubts that you have experienced? How can you see those doubts pushing you toward faith?

Prayer: Consider praying slowly through the prayer above from John Baillie.

Day 25 – Lean Not on Your Own Understanding

Our exploration this week centers around what has been called "unknowing." One of the great, classic writings about our life in Christ is titled "The Cloud of Unknowing." There are things we can know and understand, but our knowing always pales in comparison to what we can't and don't know. This leaves us in a place of tension.

We were created with minds and curiosity, and we are also dependent and vulnerable. The tension shaped by knowing and unknowing can really destabilize us. When we experience instability, we usually look for a fix. Most often that fix comes in the form of trying to get rid of the tension through either grasping for things that we can understand or just giving up. The "grasping" occurs as we settle for overly simplistic and/or incomplete theologies and worldviews. The "giving up" usually takes the form of denial, ignoring, or perhaps numbing.

The great theologian of the early church, Augustine, wrote: "God is not what you imagine or what you think you understand. If you understand, you have failed." In addition, His ways with us – the ways He companions us and loves us – are beyond understanding as well. Again, we may experience that impulse to know, but the infinite, eternal nature of God means that He is up to things that are "too wonderful" to understand. (Psalm 139:6; Job 42:3; Proverbs 30:18) That phrase "too wonderful for me" is repeated several times in the Scriptures and always in the context of what we know or don't know. It expresses a joyful acceptance that God is God ... and we are not.

Ultimately, our stabilizing comes not through our own efforts but our surrender. Jacques Philippe beautifully suggests that: "The situations that really make us grow are precisely those that we do not control." Recognizing this reality and embracing the need to wait upon God in *unknowing* is vital. For the people of Israel, their failure to wait was described simply in Numbers 21:4: "the people became impatient on the way." Waiting on God is a key feature of humility. On the other hand, our impatience reveals an insistence on knowing. Patience, waiting, and unsolved questions are frequent companions in an authentic life of faith:

"Give our Lord the benefit that His hand is leading you, and accept the anxiety of feeling yourself in suspense, and incomplete." Pierre Teilhard de Chardin

"Be patient toward all that is unsolved in your heart and try to love the questions themselves, like locked rooms and like books that are now written in a very foreign tongue. Do not now seek the answers, which cannot be given you because you would not be able to live them." Ranier Maria Rilke

Proverbs 3:5-6 are familiar, often memorized verses, and, in them, there is a wealth of counsel that often gets missed early in our journey with Christ: "Trust in the LORD with all your heart, and do not lean on your own understanding. In all your ways acknowledge him, and he will make straight your paths." Notice that we are encouraged to trust in the Lord – not our understanding of the Lord. Quite often, the truth is that we trust our understanding and that can leave us quite wobbly in seasons where our understanding is incomplete or perhaps completely shattered. The encouragement is to trust God ... to simply trust Him (not our understanding) ... to fall backward into unknowing.

To be honest, this can be a bit of a paradigm shift. And to be clear, this doesn't mean there aren't things we can know or that we should give up study and pursuit of truth. However, our studies and our pursuit of truth are secondary to and in support of our life with God. Much additional pain and consternation in a wilderness season come because we are more focused on understanding (certainty) than humble trust. The stripping of confidence in our understanding is one of the gifts of pain and suffering. What emerges is actually a deeper, more unshakable faith in God if we make that shift.

At its core, the gospel is relational not conceptual. Concepts and propositional truth stand in support of the relational realities of the gospel, and as we move into the place of unknowing, we begin to see that much in life is rooted in "both/and" (rather than "either/or") that leaves us in a dependent, trusting, humble stance. How are you clinging to your own ideas and understanding? One way to examine this is to consider what trust looks like for you. Are you trusting in a concept or is trust expressed in prayer and crying out to God? Pause here for a moment in reflective prayer. What do you notice? What is the Lord bringing to your awareness?

The response of humble trust is expressed so well in the words of David in Psalm 13. After spending time in lament – asking the question "how long?" over and over – he prays "but I have trusted in your steadfast love." In other words, *I am trusting Your love for me.* It can be a temptation to turn descriptions of what God has done in the past into promises for the future. A more honest way of interacting with our experiences as well as the text of Scripture is to realize that God promises, or guarantees, very little. What He clearly promises is: "I will never leave you nor forsake you." (Hebrews 13:5) There is no comma after this statement with a qualifying or conditional idea. There is no "He loves me if …" Simply, *I am loving you and I am with you.* Only His love, His presence, is promised and that can unfold in myriad and mysterious ways.

David Benner, in *Surrender to Love,* develops this: "Jesus is the antidote to fear. His love – not believing certain things about Him or trying to do as He commands – is what holds the promise of releasing us from the bondage of inner conflicts, guilt and terror."

Questions for reflection: how will you make the shift into trusting God rather than your understanding of God? Why is this important?

Prayer: Lord, You are so good and faithful in Your love for me. I need the courage to trust You and not simply lean on my understanding of You. Give me eyes to see Your love so that I can receive it. Thank you for meeting me where I am and leading me to Your heart and Your life. Amen.

Day 26 – Spiritual Bypassing

A subtle occurrence in our journey through life, and certainly in a wilderness season, is attributing all that is wrong or challenging or painful to external circumstances. On the other side of that coin is never acknowledging the hard things of life. These responses to life seek to short-circuit or bypass the deep soul work of the desert. Another example of trying to bypass the wilderness is using Scripture or even prayer to "spiritualize" what is going on and not interact with life as it is. We observe this in statements about God doing miracles. Of course, God *can* do miracles but perhaps the "miracle" is the medical treatment right in front of us.

This bypassing or short-circuiting can occur in different ways, usually in ways that escape our notice. The invitation is to be open to listen and notice with God ... to not bypass the place where we are. This is why spiritual practices like silence and solitude are so important. As we release our patterned responses and simply listen, we open ourselves to God in ways not polluted by bypasses. This is not easy work, and it is why Dallas Willard said, "solitude and silence are the most radical of the spiritual disciplines because they most directly attack the sources of human misery and wrongdoing ... (and) until we enter into quietness the world still lays hold of us." The sources of human misery and wrongdoing? The *sources* are generally tied up in patterned ways of bypassing reality ... whether it is *grasping for certainty* or *not trusting the presence of God*. The propensity to either positively spin difficult truth or wallow in difficult truth, rather than be with God in it, hurts us and others again and again.

For the people of Israel, we find a fascinating phrase that God uses with them multiple times in the book of Deuteronomy: "you say in your heart." (7:17; 8:17; 9:4; 15:9; 18:21; 28:67) God was graciously inviting them to look at their hearts – to notice the ways that patterns of interpreting life were often deeper than their awareness. Because we often focus on what is in our immediate awareness and modifying behaviors, we are not able to address that which is most significantly at work in shaping thoughts and behaviors. We usually want to *clean up* messes rather than *wake up* to what has produced them. This requires staying in messy places so that transformation can occur. When our pain and hurts are not transformed, they are transferred. Another way to say it is that what doesn't get healed gets passed on to others.

We see this reality played out in the prophets of the Hebrew Scriptures as Jeremiah shared God's heart for His people: "They dress the wound of my people as though it were not serious. 'Peace, peace,' they say, when there is no peace." (6:14, NIV) The picture being painted is one of bypassing: Band-Aids were being used when the wounds were much more serious, and the people said, "It's no big deal. Everything is fine." Sometimes things are a big deal. At the end of the canon of Scripture, Jesus spoke to the church in Laodicea and shared that the fruit of simply glossing over things is lukewarmness and lack of passion. (Revelation 3:14-22) He went on to share His heart and said, "I wish that you were either cold or hot." In that region of the ancient world, both hot and cold water had important uses (cold water for dying textiles and hot water for therapy). In essence, Jesus was expressing the idea that bypassing reality is useless and something that will make you sick (note the "spit you out" is a reference to vomit). To be clear, Jesus was not saying that *we* make Him sick when we bypass and short-circuit, but that the process itself is unhealthy. What were the specifics of what the church at Laodicea was doing? "For you say, I am rich, I have prospered, and I need nothing, not realizing that you are wretched, pitiable, poor, blind, and naked." (Revelation 3:17) Bypassing disconnects us from our hearts.

Are there places in your life where you find yourself tempted to say, "everything is fine"? Are there wounds or hurts in your life in which you tend to brush aside their significance and perhaps cover them with spiritual platitudes? We may find ourselves resistant to the kind of soul work that healing and transformation invite. Carl Jung made the simple observation that: "What you resist, persists."

A humble trust can unlock the courage needed to stay with the messes, hurts, and confusions. Augustine beautifully described the gift of staying in the wilderness rather than building a bridge to get out: "In my deepest wound I saw your glory, and it dazzled me."

Question for reflection: in what ways is the Lord inviting you to wake up, take off the Band-Aids, and settle into being with Him in the messes?

Prayer: Lord, I confess to you the ways that I bypass or try to cover over the messes of life. Give me the courage to trust and believe that You are with me, loving me, and shaping me. Help me settle into Your presence and grace – knowing that Your love is my healing and transformation. Amen.

Day 27 – Releasing

To put it simply, releasing is not easy. As we move away from the certainty that we have things figured out (even our own lives), humble trust and dependence may feel like it doesn't quite fit. What has worked and "fit" for so long are our attachments to strategies, things, personas, and even other people that we are now being invited to release. These attachments have seemed to protect us and give us certainty or control. However, in the wilderness, the illusions are now gone, and we begin to see that our attachments have really just protected us from love and deepening trust. Most often, those things to which we've been attached are not evil in and of themselves but when we rely upon them to provide in ways that only God can, we begin to see the problem. We may begin to notice the presence of disordered attachments, or disordered loves.

As we enter into releasing, we may begin to notice that what we believed we controlled is actually controlling us. The stripping down and loss is painful, and yet can function in a way that allows us to "detox." As we encounter strong negative reactions, we are engaging in the work of confronting those disordered attachments and it may feel like we're falling apart. In his book *Fire Within*, Thomas Dubay observed that much spiritual growth is initially discerned as backsliding. We have to be unmade and dismantled. So, in one sense, we are falling apart. This can be both confusing and painful, but the grace in experiencing those afflictive emotions is that they help us understand what needs to be released.

As the people of Israel journeyed through the wilderness, they dealt with all kinds of strong, afflictive emotional responses. To move from what was "certain" each day back in Egypt (as undesirable as living in bondage was) into this life of depending upon God to lead them was stressful. We must be careful not to downplay the difficulty of transformation … of moving from slave to free. They grumbled, they were afraid, they wept, and they were desperate. (Exodus 17, Numbers 11, 13, 14) In Numbers 14:22, God declared there were those: "who have seen my glory and my signs that I did in Egypt and in the wilderness, and yet have put me to the test these ten times and have not obeyed my voice."

Thomas Keating, in *Invitation to Love*, wrote: "As we begin the difficult work of confronting our own unconscious motivations, our emotions can be our best allies. The emotions faithfully respond to what our value system is – not what we would like for it to be, or what we think it is. Our emotions are perfect recorders of what is happening inside; hence they are the key to finding out what our emotional programs for happiness really are."

The phrase "emotional programs for happiness" is a helpful way to understand how our attachments can be disordered. These are things we've always believed will make us happy. So, rather than trying to get rid of troubling emotional responses and reactions, we learn to pay attention to them. In prayer, we ask God to give us discernment. Like lights on the dashboard of a car, emotions provide an indication that we need to check under the hood. Very simply, if we find ourselves angry, we can ask in prayer: *what is this about? What is this telling me?* In Psalm 139, we are encouraged to ask God to search our hearts. In Jeremiah 17, we see that the heart is deep and mysterious and only the Lord can truly discern.

A helpful way to think about emotions is that they were designed to proclaim what we value and protect us from what threatens what we value. Our emotions both speak to us and others. Whatever emotions are being expressed and experienced, discernment is needed to understand what is being valued. If it is joy, what am I valuing? What is my joy saying about what is important? If it is anger, am I angry over things that one should be angry about or things that are about me and getting my own way? What am I trying to protect? Am I seeking to protect good, holy things? Or is my anger protecting my emotional programs for happiness? Indeed, our emotions give us insight into the disordered attachments we need to release.

As we release what needs releasing, we are able to say with the psalmist: "Return, O my soul, to your rest; for the LORD has dealt bountifully with you." (Psalm 116:7) Notice that the foundation of returning and rest is God dealing bountifully with us. It is His grace,

His love … His attaching to us … which invites our own releasing and attaching more fully to Him. Ignatius of Loyola brilliantly commented: "Detachment comes only if we have a stronger attachment; therefore, our one dominating desire and fundamental choice must be to live in the loving presence and wisdom of Christ, our Savior."

In the prayer of Psalm 16, we observe this dynamic of releasing attachments and attaching to God. "Preserve me, O God, for in you I take refuge. I say to the LORD, 'You are my Lord; I have no good apart from you.'" (vs. 1-2) As we pray "preserve me," we are asking God to protect us rather than engaging in self-protection. As we pray "I have no good apart from you," we are proclaiming that He is the one to whom we are attaching ourselves before and above all other things. To pray "you are my Lord" is the deeply humble stance of proclaiming the God is the one we rely upon to lead our hearts. Then, our loves … our attachments … become ordered.

Stop for a moment and notice what is going on in your heart. What will it mean for God to be your Lord? Can you trust Him to lead your heart?

"When humility delivers us from attachment to our own works and our own reputation, we discover that perfect joy is possible only when we have completely forgotten ourselves. And it is only when we pay no more attention to our own deeds and our own reputation and our own excellence that we are at last completely free to serve God in perfection for God's own sake alone." Thomas Merton

Questions for reflection: how are you noticing being unmade or dismantled? What are your emotions telling you about what needs to be released?

Prayer: Lord, protect me. I take refuge in you. You are my Lord; I have no good apart from You. Amen.

Day 28 – Surrender

Earlier in the week, we touched on the element of surrender in the movement from certainty to humility. We surrender to love. We surrender to relationship with God. We surrender to being led by the One we call Lord. *Certainty* and *knowing* is about holding everything together for ourselves. It is about protecting oneself from vulnerability and not being in control. Humility opens us to a life of listening and being led by our Lord.

Eugene Peterson said it so well: "The kingdom of self is heavily defended territory. Post-Eden Adam and Eves are willing to pay their respects to God, but they don't want him invading their turf. Most sin, far from being a mere lapse of morals of a weak will, is an energetically and expensively erected defense against God."

As we explore this invitation to surrender today, let's pause for a moment and acknowledge that while we may readily give lip service to the idea of surrender, actually living as a surrendered person is another thing. In his classic song *Hold Me Jesus,* Rich Mullins sang: "Surrender don't come natural to me. I'd rather fight you for something I don't really want than to take what you give that I need. And I beat my head against so many walls and now I'm falling down ... falling on my knees."

As the people of Israel were in the process of entering into the wilderness, God said to them: "If you will diligently listen to the voice of the LORD your God, and do that which is right in his eyes, and give ear to his commandments and keep all his statutes, I will put none of the diseases on you that I put on the Egyptians, for I am the LORD, your healer." (Exodus 15:26) Notice the specific relational language in what God said: *diligently listen* and *give ear.* We often separate out obedience as being duty and put it in the context of good morality. God never does that. He invites us to relationship and then further invites us to listen to Him. From there, obedience is a relational response to God. Jacques Ellul made the observation that "Christianity is not moral, it is spiritual."

Humility is necessary in embracing a listening stance. Humility is acknowledging the reality that no matter how much I "know," I am still living in a cloud of unknowing. We feel things, perceive things, and have been shaped by things that we may trust, but the invitation of surrender is to humbly listen to the voice of God.

We see the struggle of surrender and bringing obedient response to a relational context in Jesus. As Jesus was facing the cross, He experienced the tension and struggle. "Being in an agony he prayed more earnestly; and his sweat became like great drops of blood falling down to the ground." (Luke 22:44) In the previous verses, we hear the specifics of Jesus' prayer: "Father, if you are willing, remove this cup from me. Nevertheless, not my will, but yours, be done." (vs. 42)

The way God the Son lived in human flesh is incredibly instructive when it comes to understanding surrender. Philippians 2:5-9 is a primer of sorts as we are invited to "have the mind of Christ" which is described as something already in our possession. His mind or approach to life is something that is ours in Christ. The idea of being a new creation (cf., 2 Corinthians 5:17) describes this well, but just as we may be given a new set of clothes to wear, we also have to make the decision to wear them. Notice in these verses how Jesus wore humility and responsiveness to God the Father:

> *"Have this mind among yourselves, which is yours in Christ Jesus, who, though he was in the form of God, did not count equality with God a thing to be grasped, but emptied himself, by taking the form of a servant, being born in the likeness of men. And being found in human form, he humbled himself by becoming obedient to the point of death, even death on a cross. Therefore, God has highly exalted him and bestowed on him the name that is above every name."*

The pattern described is quite compelling. First, Jesus did not consider His life (i.e., being God) as something to utilize to protect Himself. The word "grasped" is a word which means *used to one's advantage.* Instead, He emptied Himself. He released His own will, His own perspectives, and decided to be a servant. Remember that even though He is God, He took on human form with all of its vulnerabilities. He could have used His strength, power, and authority to defend and protect but instead He humbled Himself. He took on the approach of listening to and responding to God the Father.

It is easy to go back to what we know rather than wear the new garments of humility we have been given in Christ. Like Peter went back to fishing after the death of Christ (cf. John 21:1-14), we may go back to old patterns, habits, and ways of thinking. Jesus will meet us there just as He met Peter and invited him to remember. Are there ways you are tempted to retreat to what you know? As you do, reflect on what is happening, release, and remember that the Lord is with you, leading you, inviting you to surrender once again. The undoing and unravelling of moving from certainty to humility is a process, and when we notice the unravelling once again, we can smile because we are seeing with increasing clarity the ways of God in the wilderness.

"For I am about to do something new. See, I have already begun! Do you not see it? I will make a pathway through the wilderness. I will create rivers in the dry wasteland." Isaiah 43:19

Questions for reflection: what does surrender look like for you? How is the Lord shaping your understanding of surrender and inviting you to humbly surrender?

Prayer: "Take, Lord, and receive all my liberty, my memory, my understanding, and my entire will … all I have and call my own. You have given all to me. To you, Lord, I return it. Everything is yours; do with it what you will. Give me only your love and your grace, that is enough for me. Amen." Ignatius of Loyola, *The Suscipe*

Fifth Sunday
Remember God's Goodness in the Previous Week

On Sundays, we are invited to pause in order to remember God's goodness and His work in us on the journey thus far. In Psalm 106, the history of Israel's time in the wilderness is recounted and it is said that they "forgot his works" (vs. 13) and "they forgot God" (vs. 21). Remembering is vital for abiding with God on the path of love.

Use the following to engage in a time of examen prayer:
- Begin by quieting your heart before God and simply taking a few deep, slow breaths as you remember that you are in God's presence.

- Review the week with gratitude. What is the Spirit bringing to your awareness?

- Notice the ways that God has been present to you in the previous week.

- What are you thankful for? What might God want you to see that you didn't previously notice? Perhaps a place to repent?

- Select a part of your reflection from the week to pray over.

- Pray for the coming week.

Write out a prayer of thanksgiving and celebration as you look back and look forward.

Week Six

From Discontentment to Joy, v. 10

Day 29 – Secret of Being Content

A common experience in the wilderness is discontentment. We may feel discouraged, downcast, ready to throw in the towel, or even some level of depression. 1 Corinthians 10:10 encourages us "we must not grumble as some of them did and were destroyed by the destroyer." This is an intense admonition to not let our discouragement move into discontentment. Why? What's the problem with a little grumbling and complaining?

First, Paul cited the example of the Israelites when some of them were destroyed. The reference to a "destroyer" is not completely clear but is most likely a reference to angels who kept that generation from entering the land of promise. The words "destroyed" and "destroyer" demonstrate the seriousness of discontent. The numerous times they grumbled and complained throughout their wilderness journey makes it clear that this was a consequence after a *pattern* had been established. God will not force us into the transformation the wilderness can provide, and neither will He magically transform our hearts without our participation and a process.

The challenge is we often desire the magic. We want a formula. We desire to know exactly how the process works so that we can manage it and master it. God, in His gracious fathering love, desires more for us than that. He desires that we learn to be dependent and trusting.

Second, discontentment fosters a way of being in which we are not able to see or receive how God is loving us and leading us. Discontentment also steals our ability to experience joy. Quite simply, it is a miserable state. We lose out on being able to see God's love and presence because we are looking in the wrong place. A discontented heart has come to believe that happiness and joy is found in acquiring satisfaction rather than experiencing a satisfaction that is already ours in Christ.

The idea that we can acquire satisfaction is at the heart of a culture of discontent that has come to define most of western society. As we see in the people of Israel, discontent is not a modern phenomenon but there is an intensity and pervasiveness true today that rivals and perhaps surpasses anything that has come before. And, this has become the water in which we swim. Nothing is ever enough. Suffering is not supposed to happen. Undoubtedly, there is plenty in our world and in each of our lives that can lead toward discontentment. The challenge is that if we have the perspective that adding something or subtracting something from our lives will finally make us happy, we are missing the point. If we are always waiting for that next thing, saying "when I have this or that, then I'll finally be content," we will never arrive at that destination. The reality is that if you can't be happy where you are, you will not be happy anywhere.

Psalm 16:11 provides an emphatic reorientation: "You make known to me the path of life; in your presence there is fullness of joy; at your right hand are pleasures forevermore." Being present to God … this is where we find joy. With Him is satisfaction and pleasure. The psalmist describes this as the path of life … it is the way. There are times when the path of life runs right through the wilderness, but it can still be a place of joy. This is true, not because we become okay with pain in and of itself or because we deny the pain and trials, but in spite them. Wilderness can become a place of joy because it is no longer the vicissitudes of life that function as our reference point. Now, it is the presence of God and abiding in Him that becomes the lens through which we look at life. This was particularly true for the Apostle Paul as he shared in Philippians 4:11-13 that he had learned the secret to being content: "I know how to be brought low, and I know how to abound. In any and every circumstance, I have learned the secret of facing plenty and hunger, abundance and need. I can do all things through him who strengthens me." Again, it was not that he now had superhuman strength to endure all the tough things of life, but the joy of the Lord was strengthening him. Life in God's presence had become the reference point. That was the secret. This is the path of life.

As we focus this week on the movement from discontentment to joy, we'll see that joy is not something to gain or acquire but something that we begin to notice and therefore experience in God's presence. God's heart for us to depend upon Him and to trust Him is because everything for which we long is a fruit of trust and dependence. Joy is part of the fruit of entrusting ourselves to the Holy Spirit. Galatians 5:25 makes clear "if we live by the Spirit, let us also keep in step with the Spirit." We "keep in step" as we step by step, or moment by moment, live in an awareness of and attentiveness to His presence. Earlier in this portion of Scripture, we read: "But I say, walk by the Spirit, and you will not gratify the desires of the flesh." (v. 16) The implication is astounding: joyful people do not sin. When we experience joy in God's presence, we are seeing Him as we depend upon Him. If we wallow in discontent, we are not seeing Him and we open ourselves to defining life on our own terms and creating our own path.

Questions for reflection: do you believe that joy can be found in the presence of God? Don't rush too quickly past this question. Consider a specific circumstance in your life: what would it look like to see it through the lens of God's presence?

Prayer: Lord, I acknowledge that discontentment and grumbling is sometimes where I settle in the midst of difficult things. I desire to live in Your joy and be at rest. Give me eyes to look at life through the lens of Your presence. Amen.

Day 30 – Joy in the Deconstruction

In our season of distress, questions can be our downfall, but they can also be what leads us to a joyful acceptance of all that is happening in our lives. With the people of Israel, a recurring question came from their hearts as they experienced the dismantling of the wilderness: "Is the Lord among us or not?" (Exodus 17:7)

When things are not going the way we'd prefer or expect, "where is God?" is the question we can find coming from our lips. It can be an accusatory query: "God, You are clearly not involved or You obviously don't care if You would allow things like this to occur." These kinds of questions also can come from those around us as well. We find this pattern throughout the Psalms and especially in Psalm 42:

> *"My tears have been my food day and night, while they say to me all the day long, "Where is your God?" (vs. 3)*

> *As with a deadly wound in my bones, my adversaries taunt me, while they say to me all the day long, "Where is your God?" (vs. 10)*

Connecting our difficulties to the absence of God can become an automatic response because of the way we may have been formed to think about God and the way that other people talk about Him. The assumption is that *God is not involved.* Or perhaps even worse, we assume that God has withdrawn from us or is punishing us. It can be subtle or it can be quite direct, but the result is the same: we lose any sense of joy because we are believing and trusting in things that are not accurate. Further, the question can devolve into asking: what did I do wrong that I am being treated like this? Or, what do I have to do to get God back on my "good side?"

"Where is God?" is a great question when it is asked with the assumption that *God is involved* and we desire to discern His presence. Joy in the difficult season of wilderness is discovered as we view things through the lens of His presence in our lives.

Writer Paula D'Arcy stated it beautifully: "God comes to us disguised as our life." We don't "find" God in spite of our circumstances or on the "other side" of our circumstances, but in the midst of where we are. When we look at life through the lens of things being either "good" or "bad", God becomes hidden in plain sight and joy seems illusive.

What we may have missed or never been taught is that God will graciously and reliably walk us through a process of dismantling and deconstruction at some point in our journey of faith. This deconstruction often hits us in areas that we were sure we had figured out, and without the discernment that God deconstructs so He can reconstruct, we may come to the conclusion that God has abandoned us, that it is just not worth it, or that none of this "God stuff" really works. Or, we may be tempted to think that living a trusting, surrendered life is for other people but not us.

A curious, hard to understand, verse in the letter to the Philippians helps tremendously as we consider the possibility of joy and its juxtaposition with suffering. "Only let your manner of life be worthy of the gospel of Christ … and not frightened in anything by your opponents. This is a clear sign to them of their destruction, but of your salvation, and that from God. For it has been granted to you that for the sake of Christ you should not only believe in him but also suffer for his sake." (1:27–29) The wording is a bit awkward in its English translation, but the wording in Greek is "This is a clear sign to them of destruction, but to you of salvation." For many people, our suffering looks like destruction or obliteration, but for a follower of Jesus we can see it as our salvation. Paul is referring to a broader definition of salvation than being saved from hell. The salvation described is being saved from all the things we've been exploring in these weeks of Lent … being saved or delivered from expectations, independence, striving, isolation, certainty, idolatry, and the false self.

As we trust that God does these kinds of things in the wilderness, we can smile. We rejoice in our sufferings (Romans 5:3) and count it joy when we encounter trials (James 1:2). We might even say "of course, I'm in a wilderness because God loves me that much!" Indeed, hallelujah is the song of the desert. We take on a perspective that says

"I'm in for whatever it takes to experience the deliverance of God."
(*note: hallelujah means praise (halle) to (lu) Yahweh (yah)*)

So, the question "where is God?" is transformed into "where is God in this?" As we move out of discontentment to joy, we expectantly look for the ways that God is with us and how He is at work in us, and as the wilderness does its work, we may find ourselves saying, "is there anything more joyful than knowing God is at work in your life?"

"By virtue of Creation, and still more the Incarnation, nothing here below is profane for those who know how to see." Pierre Teilhard de Chardin

Question for reflection: where is God in this? Sit with that question. Listen for the Spirit's answer.

Prayer: Lord, hallelujah. I rejoice in the wilderness because I know You are at work and You are good. Amen.

Day 31 – Releasing Discontent

Experiencing contentment and joy in the wilderness may seem to be a bit unrealistic. Is it really possible to say hallelujah in the desert? At the close of the 40 years of wandering, God graciously anticipated this possible response in His words to Israel in the days leading up to their entry into the land of promise.

> *"For this commandment that I command you today is not too hard for you, neither is it far off. It is not in heaven, that you should say, 'Who will ascend to heaven for us and bring it to us, that we may hear it and do it?' Neither is it beyond the sea, that you should say, 'Who will go over the sea for us and bring it to us, that we may hear it and do it?' But the word is very near you. It is in your mouth and in your heart, so that you can do it. (Deuteronomy 30:11-14)*

What is this commandment referred to in the previous verse? *Obey the voice of the Lord, keep his commandments, and turn to the Lord your God with all you heart and with all your soul.* Certainly, this also refers to the commandment in chapter six to "love the Lord your God with all your heart, soul, and might" which is the overarching command of all the Scriptures. In addition, this describes all that we have been exploring in the previous weeks. In these verses, God is saying "you've got this. It's not unrealistic. I've been shaping you to live with me in the fullness of joy." We have a tendency to think that the promised life is far away and somewhere else – not within our grasp. However, the text goes on to say: it is not in heaven or on the other side of the ocean. When we are not present to God right where we are, we may think that the sand is better on the other side of the sea. We may think the grass is greener. All that we need to experience and enjoy life with God is present now. Jesus said something similar in Luke 17:20–21:

> *"Being asked by the Pharisees when the kingdom of God would come, he answered them, "The kingdom of God is not coming in ways that can be observed, nor will they say, 'Look, here it is!' or 'There!' for behold, the kingdom of God is in the midst of you."*

In Christ, not only is the rule and reign of God not a far-off reality, but a power and dynamic of life at work in us now. In Colossians 3:3-4, we read: "You died, and your life has been hidden with Christ in God. Whenever Christ, your life, should become manifest, then you also will become manifested with him in glory." Let these words sink in for a moment. We are hidden in Christ. A life of joy and contentment is not simply a theoretical possibility but something that is already in our possession. We experience it as we release discontentment.

The repentance process occurs as we reflect, release and remember. As you have been reflecting these last few days, how are you seeing discontentment surface in your life? Do you believe you don't have what you need? Are you tired? Are you overly busy? Are there significant stressors present? Is comparison to others a temptation?

In Hebrews 12:1-2, we are encouraged to lay some things aside in order to stay on the path that is before us:

> "Therefore, since we are surrounded by so great a cloud of witnesses, let us also lay aside every weight, and sin which clings so closely, and let us run with endurance the race that is set before us, looking to Jesus, the founder and perfecter of our faith, who for the joy that was set before him endured the cross, despising the shame, and is seated at the right hand of the throne of God."

The ultimate expression of wilderness is certainly the cross. Jesus endured the cross. He remained faithful in the midst of questions (can this cup pass from me?), stress (sweating drops of blood), abandonment (His disciples couldn't stay awake to pray), and pain (the mockery, the beatings, the cross itself). He endured or was faithful to stay on the path because of "the joy that was before him." This is an example for us because it demonstrates that the reality of joy is something that can undergird us as we seek to release. We release in order to fully experience the joy and it is joy that leads us to release. We release both *weights* and *sin*. Weights are burdens, things that encumber our journey. Put simply, sin is independence. As I think, speak, and act autonomously, it is sin. The call to lay it aside is a prompting toward dependence, a humble trusting of God.

What are the weights that are holding you down? What are those things that are leading toward discontentment? When discontent in the desert, the temptation is to take things into our own hands … to act autonomously. Where are you most tempted to autonomy? Pausing here … what do you notice? What is the Lord bringing to your awareness?

What are you being led to release? What sin will you confess? Releasing and confession lead to joy. Psalm 51:12 describes the process: "Restore to me the joy of your salvation and uphold me with a willing spirit." Psalm 25:10: "All the paths of the Lord are steadfast love and faithfulness." Again, today we come to *hallelujah*. There is a lightness and a freedom on the journey as we release all but Christ. In joy, we can proclaim that we have Christ, and He is our life. The encouragement in Deuteronomy 30 closes with:

> *"Choose life, that you and your offspring may live, loving the LORD your God, obeying his voice and holding fast to him, for he is your life and length of days, that you may dwell in the land." (vs. 19-20)*

Question for reflection: what does "choosing life" look like for you as you consider the movement from discontentment to joy?

Prayer: Lord, in the midst of so many things that could lead to discontentment, I choose You. You are my life. You are my hope. You are my joy. In each element of the wilderness, may I connect with you and abide with you in the midst of it – not denying or ignoring anything – but choosing You as the lens through which I look. Hallelujah. Amen.

Day 32 – Protecting Joy

What we behold shapes us. Our ultimate transformation will occur as "we see Him as He is" (1 John 3:2) and this gives us a window into how transformation and shaping happen in the present as well. This concept is found through the canon of Scripture. Jesus said, "The eye is the lamp of the body. So, if your eye is healthy, your whole body will be full of light." (Matthew 6:22) Proverbs 4 connects the heart with what with view: "Keep your heart with all vigilance, for from it flow the springs of life … let your eyes look directly forward, and your gaze be straight before you." (v. 23, 25) And, David, in Psalm 101 wrote: "I will not set before my eyes anything that is worthless." And, finally, we are reminded that "we all, with unveiled face, beholding the glory of the Lord, are being transformed into the same image from one degree of glory to another." (2 Corinthians 3:16)

What we behold and put before our eyes is not a minor issue in the Scriptures. It is deeply significant. If we gaze upon things other than God, we will be shaped by the culture around us, others, or even the specific circumstances in which we find ourselves. The wilderness can devastate us if we do not know how to take it all in. Of course, the answer is not to deny or ignore or escape but look at things through a different lens. If we behold without the lens of God's presence, we begin to look like the desert – dry, desperate, and desolate. As we behold God and view all through the reality of who He is, we begin to see God and see how He is at work in all things. This is certainly easier said than done, and we are challenged to be intentional so that this does not stay in the realm of words and ideas. Psalm 26 offers this encouragement: "For your steadfast love is before my eyes."

Let's examine two practical ways we can develop and deepen our "beholding." First, as the people of Israel were travelling in the wilderness, God instructed them to make specific, physical reminders of His presence and commandments for them. The phrase "out of sight, out of mind" is being addressed. When there are not specific physical reminders, we can find ourselves gazing upon almost anything without any reference to God's presence with us. Specifically, we find this encouragement in Numbers 15:37-41:

> *The LORD said to Moses, "Speak to the people of Israel, and tell them to make tassels on the corners of their garments throughout their generations, and to put a cord of blue on the tassel of each corner. And it shall be a tassel for you to look at and remember all the commandments of the LORD, to do them, not to follow after your own heart and your own eyes, which you are inclined to whore after. So you shall remember and do all my commandments, and be holy to your God. I am the LORD your God, who brought you out of the land of Egypt to be your God: I am the LORD your God."*

In addition, Deuteronomy 6 lists several encouragements to bring the commandment to love God with all your heart into every day, physical realities. God encouraged them to wear the commands and even post them on the gates to their home. He urged them to talk about the command to love when they sit down, lie down, rise up, and walk. The idea is to integrate the reality of who He is into actual, physical rhythms of our lives. What might that look like for you? Pray and ask God. Perhaps, you already have some physical reminders integrated into your life. Are they still helping you? Do you need a refresh? Finally, God says "you shall teach them to your children." A relational component to our beholding is so important. Are there ways that you are sharing and connecting with others about your life with God … His presence with you and love for you?

Frank Laubach, in the early 20th century, asked this question in *Letters by a Modern Mystic*: "Can I bring the Lord back into my mind-flow every few seconds so that God shall always be in my mind? I choose to make the rest of my life an experiment in answering this question." The challenge to have reminders and structures addresses a part of what this question is asking.

The second way we develop and deepen our "beholding" is through a contemplative seeing. This is not a physical kind of seeing per se, but a beholding in our spirit. As we develop a contemplative vision of God in our lives, it colors everything we see and behold. Then, our joy is protected as our temptation to move into discontentment wanes. We see this beautifully illustrated in Psalm 63:

> *O God, you are my God; earnestly I seek you; my soul thirsts for you; my flesh faints for you, as in a dry and weary land where there is no water. So I have looked upon you in the sanctuary, beholding your power and glory. (vs. 1-2)*

Notice the clear desert imagery in these verses: thirst, faintness, barrenness, and weariness. The response? Beholding God. Psalm 27 uses similar imagery: gazing upon the beauty of the Lord and meditating in His temple. (v. 4) This is a call to contemplative prayer. In *The Cloud of Unknowing*, we read: "Contemplation will change your heart. It will make you so kind and dynamic and loving that when you stop doing it and mingle with the world again, you'll discover that you love your slanderer as much as your friend."

The Cloud of Unknowing goes further in describing contemplative prayer: "Unclothe your awareness of analytical thoughts. Keep it empty. Don't cogitate on yourself or on others whom you know. Let them go… You no longer need to feed your mind by meditating on who you are and who God is. Grace will help you focus on holding yourself steady in the deep center of your soul, where you'll offer God the simple fact of your existence. Your spiritual affection will be filled to overflowing with love and virtue in God, who grounds you in integrity."

Questions for reflection: review the two ways that beholding can take hold in our lives. How is the Lord inviting you to behold? What might this look like in your life? Are there things you behold that you might eliminate from your life?

Prayer: Lord, I acknowledge the weariness and desolation of the desert. By Your mercy and grace, may this not lead into discontentment as I look at You, beholding Your power and glory. Amen.

Day 33 – Joy Rooted in Love

Contentment and joy are rooted in love. When we receive and experience God's love in the Spirit, joy is part of the package. The fruit of the Spirit described in Galatians 5 lists nine aspects of the fruit. Rather than describing nine separate pieces of fruit, they are referred to as a singular unit. Love could be described as the overarching description with all the other aspects being specific descriptions of the experience of love. Joy comes immediately after love on the list.

The love of God for His people is clear in the first five books of the Hebrew Scriptures. Each book was written by Moses who led the people out of slavery in Egypt. The intention of what was recorded in these books (Genesis, Exodus, Leviticus, Numbers, and Deuteronomy) was to explain how God had made a covenant with the people that He was faithfully keeping. In Genesis 12 and 15, the covenant is described as an unconditional promise. God would be faithful *no matter what*. Even as the people of Israel failed to live up to their identity as the beloved of God, God made a way for them. While pain and difficult consequences resulted from not trusting Him, He never turned His back. Over and over again, God pursued His people. He was present. He listened to their cries for help. He led them through the wilderness. While many have questioned the presence of the love of God in the Old Testament, His love is overwhelmingly present. Consider these words from Deuteronomy 7 that explain God's faithfulness to His promise:

> *"For you are a people holy to the LORD your God. The LORD your God has chosen you to be a people for his treasured possession, out of all the peoples who are on the face of the earth. It was not because you were more in number than any other people that the LORD set his love on you and chose you, for you were the fewest of all peoples, but it is because the LORD loves you and is keeping the oath that he swore to your fathers, that the LORD has brought you out with a mighty hand and redeemed you from the house of slavery, from the hand of Pharaoh king of Egypt. Know therefore that the LORD your God is God, the faithful*

God who keeps covenant and steadfast love with those who love him and keep his commandments, to a thousand generations. (vs. 6-9)

As we have explored previously, the steadfast love of God is the Hebrew word *hesed* which speaks of His loyal, faithful, pursuing love. He chooses us to be His beloved, His treasure. The reference in verse 9 to "a thousand generations" invokes a phrase from the Ten Commandments in Exodus 20:

"You shall not make for yourself a carved image, or any likeness of anything that is in heaven above, or that is in the earth beneath, or that is in the water under the earth. You shall not bow down to them or serve them, for I the LORD your God am a jealous God, visiting the iniquity of the fathers on the children to the third and the fourth generation of those who hate me, but showing steadfast love to thousands of those who love me and keep my commandments. (vs. 4-6)

While our unfaithfulness may create consequences that last for a few generations, His love extends to a thousand generations. A powerful statement is being made about God's love … it is more powerful and longer lasting than our lack of faith and trust. God's *hesed* beckons us back to Himself over and over again. A significant loss of joy occurs when we dwell upon and even define ourselves by our sin and/or lack of trust. In His love, God leads us to remember that we are His people … this is our identity. We can wallow in the discontentment of our sins and failures, or we can listen to God's voice which calls us His own … His treasure. His love and His loyalty to us is more significant than we can imagine. His love leads us into joy. No matter where we find ourselves, His love is present and preeminent. Contentment unfolds before our eyes.

Part of what we begin to notice in the desert is that as we return to God's love as our reference point, we notice God changing and shaping our heart. We notice a freedom and detachment from the conditions of the desert. This is God's work and His initiative that shapes us as we seek to be present to His love.

The great English mystic of the early 20th century, Evelyn Underhill, observed: "God is always coming to you in the Sacrament of the

Present Moment. Meet and receive Him there with gratitude in that sacrament." Receiving God's love means being able to say: *I love my life.* There is deep joy and contentment in that. Notice: we are not saying that we love the circumstances around us or what we have and don't have or what we do and don't do. We can say that we love "life" because life is not defined by all these external realities but by the love and presence of God. In this space, we are accessing deep joy. We might even be surprised by joy.

When seriously ill and living in a time of pandemic (bubonic plague) and war (100 Years War), Julian of Norwich (14th century) experienced a vision of God in which she heard Him say, "All shall be well, and all manner of things shall be well." The war started before she was born and ended after she died. The plague affected her village in England three different times. She was transformed by the love of God and experienced deep joy as Christ became her life as evidenced in the statement that "love is our Lord's meaning."

"The contemplative vision keeps before us the truth that the deepest longings of our heart were placed there by a loving God, to find their fulfillment only in relationship with God."
Geoffrey Tristram, SSJE

Questions for reflection: are you tempted to define life by the circumstances of life and your interaction with them? How might you grow in being able to say: "I love my life"?

Prayer: Lord, I can see the ways I often define my life by my failures, and yet I desire deeply to grow further into seeing life through my identity as Your beloved. I thank You for the ways that Your surprise me by joy. Amen.

Day 34 – Our Wilderness Story

As we near the end of this journey, let's revisit the concept of story. As we are able to see our story in the context of God's love, it brings healing and hope without denying the hard parts of the wilderness. When we can see our lives as part of an unfolding story, we experience joy. The joy that is discovered in the midst of pain has richness and depth as opposed to momentary or shallow joy.

Grumbling is a response to being enmeshed in the details of the story. However, our grumbling begins to fade as we take a step back and get some distance. Getting distance from the details allows us to see them in the context of the story that God is telling. When we do not see things in their context, we can misinterpret and become overwhelmed. The story that God is telling is a story of love. Love is who He is (1 John 4:8) and as Julian of Norwich said, "love is our Lord's meaning."

In Deuteronomy 6, we find the beautiful invitation that God relayed to His people through Moses: "The Lord our God, the Lord is one. You shall love the Lord your God with all your heart soul and with all your soul and with all your strength." We are likely familiar with the invitation to love but may skip over the statement that the Lord is *one*. While this statement supports the idea of monotheism, the point becomes clear as we look at the word that is used for *one*. It is the same word used in Genesis 2 to describe man and woman becoming one. *One* describes the loving, committed union of the marriage covenant. With God, it is suggesting that core to God's essence is loving union. First, we now know with the fullness of revelation that God exists in a perfect union of Father, Son, and Holy Spirit. Second, He invites us into that loving union. 2 Peter 1:3-4 tells us that "His divine power has granted to us all things that pertain to life and godliness, through the knowledge of him who called us to his own glory and excellence, by which he has granted to us his precious and very great promises, so that through them you may become partakers of the divine nature." Our response of loving God comes as we respond to the love God has shown us. "We love because He first loved us." (1 John 4:19) As we receive His loyal, faithful love, we are led to love Him and move toward deepening union and oneness with Him.

Receiving His love is rooted in seeing it. He is always loving us, but it can remain an abstract concept that is not experienced if we are not seeing it in the context of our lives. The praise and joy in the prayers of the Psalms are always rooted in recognizing specific acts of God's love. Psalm 136 begins with the words: "Give thanks to the LORD, for he is good, for his steadfast love endures forever." Then, as the story of the people of Israel is told, the phrase "His steadfast love endures forever" is connected to particular details and is repeated twenty-five more times in twenty-five verses. Today, stop for a few minutes and prayerfully read through Psalm 136.

Psalm 107 walks through various descriptions of where the people of God found themselves. *Some wandered in desert wastes, finding no city to dwell in. (v. 4) Some sat in darkness and in the shadow of death, prisoners in affliction and in irons. (v. 10) Some were fools through their sinful ways and because of their iniquities suffered affliction. (v. 17) Some went down to the sea in ships, doing business on the great waters ... He commanded and raised the stormy wind ... their courage melted away in their evil plight. (v. 23, 25, 26)* Sometimes we find ourselves in tough places through no fault of our own and sometimes we find ourselves in tough places because of the consequence of our sin. For whatever reason we end up in the wilderness, God's heart is that we would see our desperate need for Him ... that we would cry out to Him. It is not as simple as "do good" and things will go well, or "do bad" and things won't. In each situation, the people cried out to God and He was right there ... listening and loving them.

In the final verse of the Psalm, we read: *"Whoever is wise, let him attend to these things; let them consider the steadfast love of the Lord." (v. 43)* Pause for moment and consider the love of God ... the way He is meeting you or has met you in your wilderness season. How has He loved you?

Anthony DeMello describes the joy of considering God's love: "behold the One beholding you and smiling." As we perceive and receive His love, we move from discontentment toward joy because we are moving from isolated details to seeing all things in the context of His story of love. Our wilderness story becomes a love story that we wouldn't trade for the world.

Question for reflection: select a time period in your life. Take a few steps back from the details and ask God to help you see how He has loved you during that time. What do you notice in your spirit as you see His love frame the details?

Prayer: Lord, I want to see You in the circumstances of my story. Give me eyes to see and discernment to know Your love. As I perceive and receive it, may I respond by loving You with the same kind of commitment and desire with which You pursue me. Amen.

Sixth Sunday
Remember God's Goodness in the Previous Week

On Sundays, we are invited to pause in order to remember God's goodness and His work in us on the journey thus far. In Psalm 106, the history of Israel's time in the wilderness is recounted and it is said that they "forgot his works" (vs. 13) and "they forgot God" (vs. 21). Remembering is vital for abiding with God on the path of love.

Use the following to engage in a time of examen prayer:

- Begin by quieting your heart before God and simply taking a few deep, slow breaths as you remember that you are in God's presence.

- Review the week with gratitude. What is the Spirit bringing to your awareness?

- Notice the ways that God has been present to you in the previous week.

- What are you thankful for? What might God want you to see that you didn't previously notice? Perhaps a place to repent?

- Select a part of your reflection from the week to pray over.

- Pray for the coming week.

Write out a prayer of thanksgiving and celebration as you look back and look forward.

Week Seven

From Death to Life, vv. 11-13

Day 35 – The Way of the Cross   Monday

As we move into this final week of the Lenten Season, we come to the last part of the passage from 1 Corinthians 10: "Now these things happened to them as an example, but they were written down for our instruction, on whom the end of the ages has come. Therefore, let anyone who thinks that he stands take heed lest he fall. No temptation has overtaken you that is not common to man. God is faithful, and he will not let you be tempted beyond your ability, but with the temptation he will also provide the way of escape, that you may be able to endure it." (vs. 11–13)

In the examples of the people of Israel, we have considered various ways we stray off the path as we journey through the wilderness. The invitation of the wilderness is to trust the voice of love ... to trust that the pain, the disorientation, and the confusion is all used by God to deepen our souls. The temptation is to short-cut the process ... to try to escape the wilderness rather than receive it. Jesus received the wilderness that was His life (taking on human flesh) and death. The last week of His life displayed a purposed, intentional movement that mirrors the transformational process into which we are called. In Luke 9:51, we read: "When the days drew near for him to be taken up, he set his face to go to Jerusalem." He willingly entered these days that lead to the crucifixion on Friday. His life was not taken from Him, but He freely gave His life. (John 10:17-18) He could have hidden or even quietly moved on. Instead, He modeled trusting the love of the Father.

Cynthia Bourgeault suggests Holy Week is "the most sacred and mystical passage in the Christian year, when we ritually re-live and re-claim the very epicenter of Christianity, as Jesus reveals the depth of love and wagers his very life for the reality of the premise he has staked his whole ministry on: that love is stronger than death – love is the strongest power in the world ... stronger than fear — stronger than hatred – stronger than division — stronger than violence. This is the moment, this week, when we again have the opportunity in a very special way to enter into this mystery of love with him, confront our own fears and shadows, and emerge as shareholders in his resurrection — not only through faith but through our own lived experience."

In Jesus, we are given someone to follow. Jesus invited, over and over in the Gospels, with the simple words: "Follow me." This invitation is to be with Him, to trust Him, and to live like Him. This is the hope of the one who has been redeemed by grace … to be like Jesus. (Romans 8:29) 1 Peter 2:21 says: "For to this you have been called, because Christ also suffered for you, leaving you an example, so that you might follow in his steps." As Jesus walked this earth, he retraced the steps of Israel's wilderness journey with faithfulness rather than faithlessness. He became the example for us to follow in learning what it means to live faithfully … to trust God's love and presence in our lives. As we approach the cross this week … we will walk through the events of the Passion Week.

Dietrich Bonhoeffer commented: "The cross is laid on every Christian. The first Christ-suffering which every man must experience is the call to abandon the attachments of this world. It is that dying of the old man which is the result of his encounter with Christ. As we embark upon discipleship, we surrender ourselves to Christ in union with his death—we give over our lives to death. Thus, it begins; the cross is not the terrible end to an otherwise god-fearing and happy life, but it meets us at the beginning of our communion with Christ. When Christ calls a man, he bids him come and die."

This may feel quite counter-intuitive. As we think about the spiritual journey with Christ, we may think of abundant life (John 10:10) as a sweet, nice, pleasant sort of existence. By this point in our Lenten journey, I pray that you have been disabused of such a notion and are embracing the reality that abundance of life (eternal life) is found in a gritty kind of faith that transforms us into lovers from the depths of who we are. The pattern of the cross is a stripping away so that life can emerge. It is letting go of *what is* so *what can* be will emerge. All of the movements we've explored in these previous weeks can be summed up with the movement from "death to life." Jesus described this in John 12:24-25: "Truly, truly, I say to you, unless a grain of wheat falls into the earth and dies, it remains alone; but if it dies, it bears much fruit. Whoever loves his life loses it, and whoever hates his life in this world will keep it for eternal life." Jesus also put it this way: "If anyone would come after me, let him deny himself and take up his cross daily and follow me. For whoever would save his life will lose it, but whoever loses his life for my sake will save it." (Luke 9:23–24) The invitation is to *die before you die*. But there is a choice. God never forces us. He invites. He woos. He beckons. And He is always present, patient, and available to lead us.

In 1 Corinthians 10, we see a progression: humility, temptation, escape, and endurance which also marked Jesus' life. This week, we will walk through these elements of trusting God in the wilderness. Humility comes as we trust that the way of the cross is the way … as we decide not to think we know better or that perhaps there is a different, easier way. Then, we notice the temptations to hold on, to protect, to run so that we can save our life. In that noticing, we discover there is a way of escape which is most simply understood as following in the steps of Christ. Finally, we are able to endure and stay in the desert as God does His gracious work in us.

There is an intensity to the way of the cross and yet deep joy and freedom as we let go. Much of the pain, confusion, and turmoil comes as we fight and refuse the process. We can become fearful because it may seem too intense, but Jesus challenges us to see that the way of the cross is actually free and light. Matthew 11:29-30, "Take my yoke upon you, and learn from me, for I am gentle and lowly in heart, and you will find rest for your souls. For my yoke is easy, and my burden is light." His yoke, or His way, is not burdensome. It is actually "easy" which might be better translated as "well-fitting" or "free." When we release and let go of that to which we cling, we actually find freedom and that this way of the cross fits us better than we could have ever imagined.

In Jesus, we see One who knew fully what He was walking into and yet trusted the Father step by step. It is those steps we are invited to follow.

Questions for reflection: will you set your face toward Jerusalem? What fears are you noticing as we move into this final week of Lent? As you pray, what are you being asked to release? What might the Holy Spirit be asking you to surrender?

Prayer: Lord, I want to follow the way of the cross, but I am often fearful. Give me the courage to release into trusting You and the process of Your gracious, deepening work in my life. Amen.

Day 36 – Humility   Tuesday

"Let anyone who thinks that he stands take heed lest he fall." 1
Corinthians 10:12

As we walk toward the cross with Jesus, it is wise to consider these
encouragements: *are there ways that I think I am "standing"? Do I believe I
have it all figured out? Do I believe that I've got it together?* If we believe
we've got it together, we are setting ourselves up for a fall. This is
reminiscent of Proverbs 16:18, "Pride goes before destruction."

One of the consistent themes of the ministry of Jesus was the critique
and challenge of religious leaders. In our reading of the Gospels, we
may like to identify with the prodigal son, the lost coin, or the lost
sheep (cf. Luke 15), but the truth is that we often have more in
common with the older son (in the prodigal son parable) and the
religious leaders. This can be a difficult thing to consider. You may
even experience some resistance to the suggestion. Will you take a
moment and reflect on this possibility? The nature of Jesus' challenge
to the religious was that they believed they had it all figured out when
they actually were blind to spiritual realities. They had constructed
their lives in such a way that they used "religion" to hide from their
hearts – to hide from their sin. Are there ways that you hide?

All of this came to a head after Jesus entered Jerusalem when one of
the first things He did was go to the temple. In Luke 19, it is
recorded that he entered the temple and began to drive out those
who sold, saying to them, "It is written, 'My house shall be a house of
prayer,' but you have made it a den of robbers." (vs. 45-46) While
this is a very familiar event from the Gospels (all four record it), it
will be helpful to explore the background of Jesus' statement which is
made up of quotations from the Old Testament prophets Isaiah and
Jeremiah.

When a rabbi quoted the Old Testament, listeners would have heard
the verse in the context of the original statements. So, what may
seem to be a simple reference was loaded with all the power the
context supplies. First, the statement of the temple being a house of

prayer is from Isaiah 56:7. Notice the overall context: "And the foreigners who join themselves to the LORD, to minister to him, to love the name of the LORD, and to be his servants, everyone who keeps the Sabbath and does not profane it, and holds fast my covenant — these I will bring to my holy mountain, and make them joyful in *my house of prayer*; their burnt offerings and their sacrifices will be accepted on my altar; for *my house shall be called a house of prayer* for all peoples." The Lord GOD, who gathers the outcasts of Israel, declares, "I will gather yet others to him besides those already gathered." (vs. 6-8) This was a statement of God's heart for not only the people of Israel but *all* peoples to have access to Him … to be able to pray and seek Him. Second, the statement about the temple being made a den of robbers is found in Jeremiah 7:11. Again, the overall context is found in verses 8-11: "Behold, you trust in deceptive words to no avail. Will you steal, murder, commit adultery, swear falsely, make offerings to Baal, and go after other gods that you have not known, and then come and stand before me in this house, which is called by my name, and say, 'We are delivered!'—only to go on doing all these abominations? Has this house, which is called by my name, become a den of robbers in your eyes? Behold, I myself have seen it, declares the LORD." The people of Israel were going to the temple and calling out to God while they were also oppressing others and shedding the blood of others. (vs. 6)

The word "robber" in the Hebrew language of Jeremiah could be more appropriately be rendered "violent one." Jesus was accusing them of violence against others … of not giving access to the poor, the widowed, orphans, and foreigners. Further, calling the temple a "den" is a way of saying … "you have made this place a hideout." The temple (and by extension, their relationship with God) had become a place to hide … a place to ignore how they were living their faith in the world and with others. To put this into a modern context, we might say that "religious" people often do not address the way they treat others and then hide out in church singing praise songs and calling on the name of God. And don't pass too quickly over the reality that people were being oppressed. Are there ways that you actively or (more likely) passively are involved in the oppression of others?

Before you react with, *I don't do that,* are you willing to stop and consider a few questions? Do you ever use God as a hideout … a way to make yourself feel better … but leave sin in your life unaddressed? Can you humble yourself and acknowledge ways that you praise God on the one hand and then ignore sin on the other? Are you open to looking at ways that you are part of things that oppress others? Are there systems in place around you that it is easy to ignore because you benefit from them?

We are plunged into a wilderness season to lay bare the reality of our lives … to come out of hiding. This demonstrates the grace of a wilderness season. When the circumstances of our lives are pleasant, we may not pay attention. Can you come out of hiding? It requires trusting the grace of God … trusting that we will be safe. Simone Weil wrote "Grace fills empty spaces, but it can only enter where there is a void to receive it." This illustrates the need for faith and trust. We may not feel safe or experience grace in those places where we are holding on and not releasing our sin. And then, when we do, grace comes flowing in.

In his book *Addiction and Grace,* Gerald May discussed this reality in taking about things being "stripped away, leaving a desert like spaciousness where my customary props and securities no longer existed. Grace was able to flow into this emptiness, and something new was able to grow." In this event from Jesus' last week, we are encouraged to empty our hands … to let the desert expose things hidden.

Questions for reflection: sit with what you are noticing being stirred in your spirit. Ask the Lord to search your heart. What is coming to your awareness? How is God calling you out of hiding?

Prayer: Lord, I humble myself and acknowledge the ways I have praised You on the one hand and not treated others with justice and equity on the other. Thank you for the grace to let go of those things and the experience of grace that flows as I do. Amen.

"No temptation has overtaken you that is not common to man. God is faithful, and he will not let you be tempted beyond your ability, but with the temptation he will also provide the way of escape, that you may be able to endure it." 1 Corinthians 10:13

As we come out of hiding, we are invited to be a "house of prayer." (Luke 19:46) Our lives are designed to embody prayer as a way of life. It is our identity, our calling, our joy. And yet, the intimacy and emptiness of the *wilderness* way of the cross may confuse us.

The temptation is that we might resist or avoid the releasing and letting go required for following Jesus to the cross. As we consider the cost of taking up our own crosses, we can be tempted to look for an easier way. We may find ourselves drawn to the fruit of a life in Christ, and yet not sure if we really want to lay down our lives. For most of us, we've spent years constructing a life that we perceive will keep us safe … and that all falls apart in the wilderness. As we begin to stabilize in a wilderness season, we find ourselves drawn to move into the fullness of a humble, surrendered, dependent life, and yet the temptation to return to those old strategies of protecting ourselves may become quite fierce.

It's not that the temptation is necessarily stronger, but we are aware like never before and it seems more significant. The choice is laid out before us.

Peter was confronted with this same choice as He walked with Jesus during this final week. Previously, Peter boldly expressed His desire to follow Jesus and leave everything behind. (cf., Matthew 19:27) He also expressed some misunderstanding when he "rebuked" Jesus and said, "This shall never happen to you." (Matt 16:22) During that week, as the pressure to fully embrace the way of the cross mounted, we see Peter resisting and avoiding. He resisted as he cut off the ear of the Roman guard (John 18:10) even though Jesus had told him that the Son of Man must suffer and be rejected (Luke 9:22). Peter avoided the issue as we read that he followed at a distance (Mark 14:54) which then led to a denial that he even knew Jesus.

Are there ways that you are fighting against the forces that threaten your safety? Are there places where you are following at a distance?

Perceiving that our ways of existing in the world are threatened by the cross is both a necessary discernment as well as a normal experience. If we don't feel that threat, we probably aren't paying attention. Jesus made it quite clear, but it often only reaches to the depths of our heart when in the wilderness and face to face with the loss: "If anyone would come after me, let him deny himself and take up his cross and follow me. For whoever would save his life will lose it, but whoever loses his life for my sake will find it. (Matthew 16:24–25) Certainly, Peter felt his way of life slipping away as he saw the guards coming after Jesus and as he was confronted by the crowd. And this is where the temptation comes in.

If it will cost us something, we are tempted to look for an easier way. The statement that there is no temptation that has not been common to man is meant to encourage and also to humble. These temptations are normal and something we can expect. Discerning the presence of avoidance and resistance in our spiritual journey is vital. Otherwise, we may find ourselves swept off the path without even realizing what is going on.

Avoidance tends to be a bit more passive and shows up in a lack of honesty or a lack of awareness of our internal world. We end up staying in our heads and ignoring our heart as a way of ignoring the cost of following Jesus. We might employ avoidance in order to not deal with the very real pain we've experienced or are experiencing. Part of the temptation of avoidance is that we may cloak it in the religious garb of platitudes ("God is good … all the time" or "I just need to trust"), of correct theology, or of right behavior.

Avoidance often has particular expressions based on our temperaments and giftings. We may feel the need to avoid anger, needs, failure, ordinariness, emptiness, doubt, pain, weakness, or conflict. Can you see yourself in any of these things? Are you willing to ask the Lord to search your heart? How do you perceive these kinds of avoidance "protecting" you from the suffering of taking up your cross?

Resistance is the more active expression of the temptation to deny the suffering of the cross. We flat out say "no" or we refuse to engage in the kind of deep soul work that is necessary in the desert. Again, we might wrap our resistance in optimism ("everything is fine"), moralism (we go to behavior modification), or spiritualizing. Interestingly, Henry David Thoreau observed: "The path of least resistance leads to crooked rivers and crooked men."

In any kind of avoidance or resistance, we are asking: *how do I stay safe?* When we ask that question, we are actually trying to be safe from having to follow Christ. The fullness of life in Christ is found as we die to self … as we choose to love. As Carl Trueman put it, "Much of life can be explained as an attempt to deny or escape from death." The intimacy and emptiness of the wilderness threaten our previous understandings of how life should work.

Getting the "Egypt" out of us requires time and patience. The layers of resistance and avoidance that can build up over time have to be peeled away layer by layer. And in it all, God abides with us in grace … tenderly, gently, and persistently inviting us to sit still and submit ourselves to His surgeon's scalpel.

Question for reflection: how do I see the temptation to avoid in my life? What does resistance look like for me? Sit in quiet trust and ask the Lord to give insight into these things.

Prayer: "Almighty God, whose most dear Son went not up to joy but first He suffered pain, and entered not into glory before He was crucified: Mercifully grant that we, walking the way of the Cross, may find it none other than the way of life and peace; through Jesus Christ our Lord, who lives and reigns with You and the Holy Spirit, one God, forever and ever. Amen." (*Book of Common Prayer*)

"but with the temptation he will also provide the way of escape, that you may be able to endure it." 1 Corinthians 10:13

The overall temptation in the wilderness is to escape, to run, to get out. It is a natural instinct, but as we have seen, God desires to be with us in the wilderness and He has His good purposes for how He shapes us in the desert. When frustrated, it is indeed tempting to say: *I'm done. I'm out of here.* At that point, we experience the temptation to manufacture a way of escape.

It is a grace when we begin to notice our impulse to escape. At that point, we have an opportunity to stop, slow down, and notice how God is at work and what He is doing. In 1 Corinthians 10:13, we are encouraged that God provides an escape as well, but the escape is from the temptation to escape the situation, not the situation itself. This brings us back once again to a concept we explored earlier in this Lenten journey: it is not about **getting out**, but trusting God **in** the wilderness. In the mysterious depths of God's love, giving us an escape hatch from the situation is much less loving than giving us an escape from the temptation to escape. The point of being rescued from the temptation is that we would be able to endure … remain … hold fast.

As we come to this final day before Jesus would be crucified, the temptation to escape was perhaps never more heightened. But rather than run, Jesus kept walking step by step, being led by the Father. How He interacts with those around Him speaks volumes about the nature of the "escape from temptation."

The first words of the description of this final night are often skipped over but notice the profound nature of what is expressed: "Now before the Feast of the Passover, when Jesus knew that his hour had come to depart out of this world to the Father, having loved his own who were in the world, he loved them to the end." (John 13:1) He loved them to the end! Consider that for a moment. Rather than being self-focused and self-protective, He loved. Don't miss the reality that Jesus existed in human flesh and was facing a gruesome death ... and He loved them to the end. For us, the reflex under stress is usually to retreat, regroup, and devise a strategy for survival. Jesus walked toward His death with love. We are invited to follow in those footsteps.

The "escape" that God provides is not a strategy built around survival but love. Rather than retreating inward, we are invited to move out ... to move into love. Jesus was immersed in the love of the Father which then directed His "strategy" for moving through the most challenging day of His life. As we "die before we die," we are freed to leave the details of our earthly existence to the good purposes of the Father rather than pouring ourselves into survival strategies. As we consider the movement this week of "death to life," we begin to see that survival mode is a kind of death and as we release it we are ushered into life ... a life defined by and directed by the love of God.

Jesus clearly expressed this love in washing the feet of His disciples as they moved toward the Passover meal together. Imagine: on the most difficult night of His earthly existence, He stopped, stooped, and served. He entrusted all of Himself to God the Father and loved others to the very end.

Then, in the context of this meal – which He clearly connected to His impending sacrificial death – He shared that all of His disciples would fall away. How He handles this is another staggering expression of love. He isn't angry but simply says, "Don't worry; I'll see you in Galilee." (Matthew 26:30-32) He wanted to prepare them and let them know that He knew and would still be there for them. He displayed incredible grace and provision even as He shared with Peter that He knew Peter would deny Him. He was preparing them all and considered them before Himself. As we entrust ourselves to God, we are freed to love. And so, this is the "escape" from the temptation to escape.

Finally, the dinner itself is a testimony that the way of the cross is the way of love. Ann Voskamp made the observation: "On the night Jesus was betrayed — He gave thanks." She went on to say: "On the night when the prodigal sliced open your heart, on the night when you lost your job, when your person slammed out the door, and the toilet stopped flushing, and the dog gagged and puked all over the back mat, on the night when it looked like the dawn would never come again — there is always a choice, and why not choose what Jesus did? Because when Jesus had to fight through dark, staring right into the most impossible situation of the Cross — what does He do? Out of a universe of supernatural options at the tip of His fingers — what does Jesus do? On the night when Jesus was betrayed — He gave thanks. If Jesus can give thanks in that — you can give thanks in everything."

Sit with that for a few moments. How does "dying before you die" free you to love and give thanks? What is stirring in your heart and mind as you consider Jesus' steps on this Thursday night before the crucifixion?

Episcopal brother James Koester summarizes the invitation: "The way we are invited to walk is not an easy one. It involves towel, basin, and water. It requires us to bend, to stoop, and to kneel. It involves cross and nails, thorns and spear. It requires us to die. It involves tomb, and grave clothes. It requires us to lay everything aside, even our own lives. But for those who follow, it is life, and peace, and joy."

Question for reflection: how is God shaping you and speaking to your heart?

Prayer: Lord, here I am in the middle of the wilderness and I notice my instinct for survival and self-protection, and I also notice my desire to follow the way of Jesus. Strengthen me through the Holy Spirit to release self-preoccupation and receive the grace to walk in love, to give thanks, to serve others. Amen.

Day 39 – Endurance   Friday

"… that you may be able to endure it." 1 Corinthians 10:13

Friday … the most horrific day in human history as God in human flesh was brutally crucified. Yet, *this* Friday has been called *good*. Good … a word that is often flippantly thrown around to modify any number of things. And yet, that Friday was good. It is was good in the most true, pure, solid, holy way possible.

"God shows his love for us in that while we were still sinners, Christ died for us." (Romans 5:8)

His love for us displayed perfectly. And at the same time, this day was devastating for those first followers of Jesus. They were disoriented and displaced in the depths of wilderness. Confusion, doubt, despair, loss, and fear all mixed together. As we refuse to run from the suffering, we find ourselves in a waiting space … a liminal reality in which is can be difficult to know if it is day or night. The invitation in the desert season is *trust* which leads us to stay in that liminal space. This is what Paul refers to as "endurance" in 1 Corinthians 10. As we wait, we remain present and stay open to the work of God.

While the questions may be fast and fierce, we wait with God in trust … knowing that He is at work when we can't see it. Even though they were told that this would happen, the disciples couldn't piece it together. It was too much. It couldn't fit into any of their categories. There was nothing about love, peace, and hope that seemed to connect with their Rabbi and Lord hanging on a cross. While we can see the whole picture in retrospect, it wasn't so clear in the throes of such suffering. And so it is with us in our wilderness. Because we have the cross and resurrection as the center of faith, we can borrow from this paradigm to fuel our trust. Death to life (cross to resurrection) is the pattern. It is how God works.

Of course, we think: can't there be an easier way? This was, of course, Jesus' question in the Garden of Gethsemane the night before. (Luke 22:42) Anne Lamott suggests: "Faith includes noticing the mess, the emptiness, and discomfort, and letting it be there until some light returns." Staying in the hurt, confusion, and pain allows the space for a shaping ... a transformation. As we stay in the pain that our crosses produce, we are able to see the grace and provision of God.

When Jesus spoke with Nicodemus in John 3, He said something that drew upon the forty years in the wilderness: "And as Moses lifted up the serpent in the wilderness, so must the Son of Man be lifted up, that whoever believes in him may have eternal life." (vs. 14–15) While it might have been a bit opaque in the moment, Jesus was clearly connecting the bronze serpents of Numbers 21 to the cross. What was happening in Numbers?

> *From Mount Hor they set out by the way to the Red Sea, to go around the land of Edom. And the people became impatient on the way. And the people spoke against God and against Moses, "Why have you brought us up out of Egypt to die in the wilderness? For there is no food and no water, and we loathe this worthless food." Then the LORD sent fiery serpents among the people, and they bit the people, so that many people of Israel died. And the people came to Moses and said, "We have sinned, for we have spoken against the LORD and against you. Pray to the LORD, that he take away the serpents from us." So Moses prayed for the people. And the LORD said to Moses, "Make a fiery serpent and set it on a pole, and everyone who is bitten, when he sees it, shall live." So Moses made a bronze serpent and set it on a pole. And if a serpent bit anyone, he would look at the bronze serpent and live. (vs. 4–9)*

Grace in the wilderness. Provision. And it required a trusting look – what Jesus calls belief in John 3. Can you believe that God is at work in your worst moments? Can you trust that what looks like the worst thing imaginable will soon be called good? Can you trust? Death always leads to resurrection. Always. Every time. Without exception.

In Christ, Sunday is always two days away. We experience losses (deaths) in this life that God uses to transform us in deeper and deeper experiences of His love. And, when we experience our ultimate death, God uses that to transform us as well. This is why the Apostle Paul can say that "nothing can separate us from the love of God." (Romans 8) When we settle into that reality, we are free. We are free to experience the pattern of death to life over and over again. And so, even in the pain and uncertainty, a little smile may emerge because of the knowledge that God is doing what He does.

The gospel writer John, who was also one of Jesus' twelve disciples, referred to Himself as the disciple whom Jesus loved. (John 13; John 18; John 19; John 21) Certainly, Jesus loved all the disciples, but John's identity as the beloved had been shaped so deeply that this is how he saw Himself. It is significant to note that when all the other disciples scattered as Jesus was arrested, tried, and taken to the cross, John endured … He stayed … He remained. He stayed in the pain and He experienced the love of Jesus in more profound ways than anyone else. His first New Testament letter is rooted in discussing the love of God. He wrote the statement: "God is love." (1 John 4:8) He is love, and this is our trust in the wilderness.

It is His love that transform a disastrous Friday into a good one. Will you look at the cross and let it encourage you to endure? He is at work even as our world falls apart.

Question for reflection: how is God stirring your heart? What is He inviting on this Good Friday?

Prayer: Lord, as I look at the cross, I trust that just as the serpents in the wilderness were transformed into a healing agent, You take it all and transform it into healing and life. I look to the cross and believe. I know that in Him is life. Amen.

Day 40 – Waiting   Saturday

And then we wait.

The work is done, and now we wait in humble, enduring trust.

On this Saturday, it is quiet. The intensity of Friday is no longer. The quiet, mixed with lingering questions, provides a different kind of intensity. Saturday may feel a bit dark. The suffering of the wilderness is a companion of sorts, and then the quietness of waiting companions us in a different way. Over the centuries, one of the most significant descriptions of silence and waiting is *dark night of the soul*. A dark night of the soul is an experience of forsakenness. We may hear echoes of "My God, My God, why have you forsaken me?" (Matthew 27:46; Psalm 22:1)

A dark night of the soul is not the suffering itself but the silence that is present as we wait for something new, something unrevealed. The silence can be deafening unless we are able to rest into it, knowing that the pattern of *death to life* is surely at work. For the people of Israel, they understood there was a destination. They still struggled. For the disciples on that first Saturday between cross and resurrection, there was apparently a measure of disbelief. The disciples from Emmaus made their preparations to head back home. (cf. Luke 24:13) The eleven gathered together and had hardened their hearts. (cf. Mark 16:14)

As we walk through our own wilderness, we may find ourselves in a place of disbelief ... even hardening our hearts ... struggling to keep an open, trusting heart. In these moments, we may become aware that we have been trusting our own understanding rather than trusting God Himself. We want to know ... to grasp what is happening! On Saturday, we know very little, if anything at all. We are invited to pray a prayer like "I don't understand you, but I trust you." (Basilea Schlink)

In Psalm 22, the words that follow the cry of feeling forsaken are these: "Yet you are holy, enthroned on the praises of Israel. In you our fathers trusted; they trusted, and you delivered them. To you they cried and were rescued; in you they trusted and were not put to shame."

Pausing here for a moment: in the darkness of Saturday, can you let go of understanding and move toward trust? Don't move along too quickly. Feel the weight of not knowing and rest in the One who does know ... the One who holds your life. Can you sit with that word "yet" from Psalm 22? This leads us into a freedom in the empty space that makes what is coming even more profound.

Jacques Philippe, in *Interior Freedom,* suggests: "It is natural and easy to go along with pleasant situations that arise without our choosing them. It becomes a problem, obviously, when things are unpleasant, go against us, or make us suffer. But it is precisely then that, in order to become truly free, we are often called to choose to accept what we did not want, and even what we would not have wanted at any price. There is a paradoxical law of human life here: one cannot become truly free unless one accepts not always being free! To achieve true interior freedom, we must train ourselves to accept, peacefully and willingly, plenty of things that seem to contradict our freedom. This means consenting to our personal limitations, our weaknesses, our powerlessness, this or that situation that life imposes on us, and so on."

On this in-between day, reflect on the ways that you are in-between ... incomplete ... unknowing. You are in this place because something has died. You have been led to stop fighting, stop avoiding, stop resisting. Now, you accept the emptiness because it means that God has graciously allowed death. As you prepare today for resurrection, remember that resurrection is meaningful because something has died. Hold onto that hope in order to fully experience the hope of Sunday.

Thomas Merton wrote, "No despair of ours can alter the reality of things or stain the joy of the cosmic dance which is always there ... we are invited to forget ourselves on purpose, cast our awful solemnity to the winds and join in the general dance." Today, we wait at the edge of the dance floor in trust and in hope, and tomorrow we dance. Perhaps, we tap our foot a bit even today as we know what is coming.

Question for reflection: today, simply reflect on where you are in the movement from "death to life." What is it like to be in the in-between? In this space, can you pray: "yet you are holy?"

Prayer: "God, I so much want to be in control. I want to be the master of my own destiny. Still, I know that you are saying: 'Let me take you by the hand and lead you. Accept my love and trust that where I will bring you, the deepest desires of your heart will be fulfilled.' Lord, open my hands to receive your gift of love. Amen." (Henri Nouwen)

Resurrection Sunday – Called You by Name

But Mary stood weeping outside the tomb, and as she wept she stooped to look into the tomb. And she saw two angels in white, sitting where the body of Jesus had lain, one at the head and one at the feet. They said to her, "Woman, why are you weeping?" She said to them, "They have taken away my Lord, and I do not know where they have laid him." Having said this, she turned around and saw Jesus standing, but she did not know that it was Jesus. Jesus said to her, "Woman, why are you weeping? Whom are you seeking?" Supposing him to be the gardener, she said to him, "Sir, if you have carried him away, tell me where you have laid him, and I will take him away." Jesus said to her, "Mary." She turned and said to him in Aramaic, "Rabboni!" (which means Teacher).   *John 20:11-16*

He blesses every love that weeps and grieves
And now he blesses her who stood and wept
And would not be consoled, or leave her love's
Last touching place, but watched as low light crept
Up from the east. A sound behind her stirs
A scatter of bright birdsong through the air.
She turns, but cannot focus through her tears,
Or recognize the Gardener standing there,
She hardly hears his gentle question, 'Why,
Why are you weeping?', or sees the play of light
That brightens as she chokes out her reply,
'They took my love away, my day is night.'
An then she hears her name, she hear Love say
The Word that turns her night, and ours, to Day.

Easter dawn. a sonnet by Malcolm Guite

"But now thus says the LORD,
he who created you, O Jacob,
he who formed you, O Israel:

154

'Fear not, for I have redeemed you;
I have called you by name, you are mine.'"
Isaiah 43:1

Prayerfully reflect for a few minutes on the One who calls you by name. Imagine that you were there on that first Easter morning looking for Jesus. He calls you by name. How do you respond?

As we come to the end of this Lenten journey in the wilderness, we also come to a beginning. What will you leave behind? What will you take with you as you continue to journey with Jesus into this next season of your life with Him?

Finally, remember that you have been brought from death to life in Christ. "You died, and your life has been hidden with Christ in God. Whenever Christ, your life, should become manifest, then you also will become manifested with him in glory." (Colossians 3:3-4) This pattern continues to be **the** pattern. Notice and participate with God in what He is doing in taking you from death to life over and over again. In Christ, you have the "working of His great might that He worked in Christ when He raised Him from the dead and seated Him at His right hand in the heavenly places." (Ephesians 1:19-20)

"… for behold, the winter is past; the rain is over and gone. The flowers appear on the earth, the time of singing has come, and the voice of the turtledove is heard in our land."
Song of Solomon 2:11–12

Lord, thank You for loving me and calling me by name in the middle of the wilderness. Thank You for the resurrection power at work in me. Give me eyes to see it and join in what You are doing. I trust You. I love You. I praise Your holy name. Amen.

Appendix 1

Dates of Lent

Year	Ash Wed	Good Friday	Easter
2022	2-Mar	14-Apr	17-Apr
2023	22-Feb	7-Apr	9-Apr
2024	14-Feb	29-Mar	31-Mar
2025	5-Mar	18-Apr	20-Apr
2026	18-Feb	3-Apr	5-Apr
2027	10-Feb	26-Mar	28-Mar
2028	1-Mar	14-Apr	16-Apr
2029	14-Feb	30-Mar	1-Apr
2030	6-Mar	19-Apr	21-Apr
2031	26-Feb	11-Apr	13-Apr
2032	11-Feb	26-Mar	28-Mar
2033	2-Mar	15-Apr	17-Apr
2034	22-Feb	7-Apr	9-Apr
2035	7-Feb	23-Mar	25-Mar
2036	27-Feb	11-Apr	13-Apr
2037	18-Feb	3-Apr	5-Apr
2038	10-Mar	23-Apr	25-Apr
2039	23-Feb	8-Apr	10-Apr
2040	15-Feb	30-Mar	1-Apr

About the Author
Ted Wueste

Dr. Ted Wueste is husband to
Jenifer and father to two adult
children. Living in the foothills
of the desert mountain preserve
in Phoenix, Arizona, he embraces
a desert kind of spirituality as he
encounters God and seeks to
pastor through spiritual direction,
writing, blogging, and directing
the Spiritual Formation Society
of Arizona.

Having pastored in a local church for over 25 years, Ted's heart and
focus in ministry has shifted to creating safe spaces for leaders in
ministry to encounter God in increasingly intimate ways.

You can learn more about Ted, read blogs, and find other resources
at desertdirection.com as well as sfsaz.org.

Other works by author …

Mansions of the Heart Study Guide (with Tom Ashbook)
The Practice of the Presence of God Study Guide
Let Every Heart Prepare Him Room: Advent Reflections
Que Cada Corazon Prepare Lugar Para El: Reflexiones de Adviento
Welcome Everything: Reflections on a Journey Through Cancer

Made in the USA
Las Vegas, NV
24 February 2022